Creative Curriculum
Leadership

For Lara

Creative Curriculum Leadership

Dale L. Brubaker

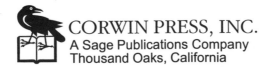

CORWIN PRESS, INC.
A Sage Publications Company
Thousand Oaks, California

For information address:

Corwin Press, Inc.
A Sage Publications Company
2455 Teller Road
Thousand Oaks, California 91320

SAGE Publications Ltd.
6 Bonhill Street
London EC2A 4PU
United Kingdom

SAGE Publications India Pvt. Ltd.
M-32 Market
Greater Kailash I
New Delhi 110 048 India

Printed in the United States of America

Library of Congress Cataloging-in-Publication Data

Brubaker, Dale L.
    Creative curriculum leadership / Dale L. Brubaker.
        p. cm.
    Includes bibliographical references and index.
    ISBN 0-8039-6140-5 (cl. : alk. paper).—ISBN 0-8039-6141-3
    (pb. : alk. paper)
        1. Curriculum planning—United States. 2. Curriculum change—
    United States. 3. Educational leadership—United States.
    I. Title.
    LB2806.15.B78 1994
    375'.001'0973—dc20
                                                                          93-45689
                                                                              CIP

97 98 10 9 8 7 6 5 4 3 2

Corwin Press Production Editor: Rebecca Holland

Contents

Foreword

Creative Curriculum Leadership is a unique and useful addition to the curriculum literature. The book deals with the process dimensions of curriculum development through the prism of creative imagination and self-expression. The major underlying theme is that personal growth and professional development are symbiotic functions in tandem, which mutually nurture one another.

Among other things, the volume provides a vivid portrait of the ways in which creative inspiration and idealism can order and direct a vision of learning. In clear, concise, easily grasped arguments, the chapters demonstrate how each of us can use our talents and enterprise to improve the human lot. The infrastructure of the text is based upon self-understanding, evolution, sensitivity to human settings, and the sequential cultivation of capacity and capability.

Philosophers have long posited that proper human action ought rightly to vary according to circumstance and situation. Because the motives underlying behavior are individually determined, psychologists fault the efforts of social scientists to devise a general theory of human action. As we engage in life, we not only make private moral determinations, but also tend to base our tactics on the conditions that prevail. So it is, seemingly, in schooling. There is no way to avoid either the benefits or the liabilities of free human action. Clearly, leaders should enable teachers to deepen their perceptions, increase their awareness, perfect their skills, and sharpen their sense of purpose. All of these, however, should not constitute a universal prescription. Just as the physician must qualify the use of a drug, even within the range of standard practice, because it may not be appropriate in a particular situation, so must we make allowances for exceptions to standard practice in curriculum.

The downfall of much of the recent reform has, in large measure, been a consequence of faulty innovative process. Lesson plans, courses of study, standards and assessment, and policies are literally at the mercy of the teacher. At best they are means to an end. If they are to be useful, the teacher must like them, value their utility, and master the intricacies of their use. Thus the wise leader recognizes that the teacher is the indispensable agent of curriculum reform.

Skillfully enhanced through a series of vignettes and case studies, the ideas set forth on the pages that follow are as much a treatise on leadership as curriculum activity, and rich in practical illustration. In distinguishing between education based upon inner conviction and that based upon outer conviction, the author's conviction is that coherent diversity, enlivened by the free spirit, can provide helpful alternatives to that which is scripted. In a time when formula and mandate threaten to dominate educational policy, the author's convictions provide a badly needed reminder that teaching should be a helping profession; that warmth, compassion, and common sense offer more virtue than blind obedience to one dogma or another; and that liberating vision stems from both the open eye and the open mind.

LOUIS J. RUBIN

Preface

The newly elected superintendent of a large school system in the Midwest called his central office staff together and briefly introduced them to his view of curriculum:

> We need to identify those schools with low test scores after which we will do what needs to be done to bring about an incremental positive change in the scores. Because you as curriculum leaders are in charge of the curriculum and the testing program, I will hold you accountable for raising the test scores. I will give you the funds to raise the scores. If you are successful there will be plenty of money for you to attend conferences of your choice; if you are not, you will stay at home. Higher test scores will make us appear to be winners. I want to look like a winner.

We can certainly not fault the superintendent for sending unclear signals to central office leaders. He made known a tangible outcome for schools—raise test scores. And he implicitly defined curriculum as a body of knowledge and skills to be ingested by students in order to raise such test scores. We need to remind ourselves that test construction and distribution are a major component of curriculum construction and distribution. This is very big business. M. Scott Peck (1993, p. 232) uses the term *product vocation* to describe such ventures. Curriculum development, according to this superintendent, means the technical creation of plans of study, which when taught effectively will raise test scores. His approach to curriculum is outside-in: An outside stimulus (curriculum) is efficiently applied to an inside target (central office leaders, teachers, and students) so that a desirable response (higher test scores) will make all concerned appear to be winners. The essentially political nature of the superintendent's approach to these matters is revealed in his top-down governance style, a bureaucratic model for governance: (1) anticipate public reaction; (2) make the decision; and (3) implement the decision (Brubaker, 1982). Numbers, as revealed in higher test scores, make the superintendent appear to be a winner, and for their successful efforts central office leaders will be rewarded with resources to attend conferences. If central office leaders are not successful, they will be punished by having their travel funds cut.

The effect, intended or unintended, of the superintendent's approach to curriculum is to dehumanize the setting. Sociologist Max Weber describes this process:

> [Bureaucracy by] its special nature develops the more perfectly the more bureaucracy is "dehumanized," the more completely it succeeds in eliminating from official business love, hatred, and purely personal, irrational, and emotional elements which escape calculation. This is the specific nature of bureaucracy. (Gerth & Mills, 1946, pp. 215-216)

Gloria Steinem (1992, pp. 33-34) states this in a more personal way: "Hierarchies try to convince us that all power and well-being come from the outside, that our self-esteem depends on obedience and measuring up to their requirements."

What price do we pay for this dehumanization? We deny ourselves the opportunity to directly encounter other persons. Instead of participating in the creative process, "we worship technique . . . as a way of evading the anxiety of the direct encounter" (May, 1975, p. 101). And those who define their roles primarily as political also pay a price. Hedrick Smith (1988, p. 92) describes this price: "Politicians strike me as a lonely crowd, making few deep friendships because almost every relationship is tainted by the calculus of power: How will this help me?"

Let us now turn to an assistant principal in the South who has a different view of curriculum, one that entertains creativity in herself and others, and in the process involves her in the anxiety of the direct encounter. Denise Hedrick is being interviewed for a middle school principalship. The first question she is asked is "What are three keywords that describe you?" She replies as follows:

> I have been recently undergoing a change in my value system, in large part because of my reading Stephen Covey's *The Seven Habits of Highly Effective People*. This book has had a profound effect on me, and I am now in the process of evolving a new way of looking at myself, from the inside out. So to answer your question, the first keyword that describes me is authentic. The second keyword is integrity, which includes being honest, keeping promises and fulfilling expectations. The third keyword is proactive—taking the initiative to make things happen. What I really want to do as a leader is to create win-win situations. I know it takes time to do this but it pays off in the long run as opposed to rushing in and trying to fix things in a hurry.
>
> I have demonstrated as an assistant principal that I can make tough decisions in relating to various publics, but many diffi-cult problems can be avoided through preventive actions. I can be very task oriented but the quality of the task performed depends on the quality of the person within.
>
> Sometimes I feel like Dorothy in *The Wizard of Oz*. I traveled so far only to find out that the answers were inside of me all along. My paradigm has shifted from focusing on the light that is directed at me, to focusing on the light that shines within me. Gloria Steinem, author of *Revolution from Within*, helped me see that there is a difference between core self-esteem and situational self-esteem. As a result, I have a new clarity of purpose and a personal mission statement. Character is at the center of good leadership. (Hedrick, 1993)

The two approaches to leadership previously described force us to confront a major contradiction facing educational leaders in the

United States today. External pressures are leveled at educators from many sides, but to simply structure one's life in reaction to such pressures is to feel hollow within. The situational self-esteem afforded by higher tests scores and other measures that make one *appear* to be a winner do little for the educator's core self-esteem. At the same time, however, the educational leader needs the political skills to realistically deal with external pressures.

In giving leadership seminars across the country, I have encountered a tremendous sense of sadness and a thirst for creativity and self-expression in relating to the contradiction described in the previous paragraph. Teachers and administrators want to nurture the sense of awe, wonder, and amazement, which they experienced as curious children, turned on to the world around them (Sarason, 1993a). And yet, they feel beaten down by external pressures that seek the quick fix. This same contradiction is evident in teacher and administrator preparation programs in colleges and universities (Sarason, 1993b).

The aim of *creative curriculum development* is to squarely face this contradiction and then shed light on ways in which today's educators can creatively lead others confronted by the same dilemma. In the process of meeting this aim, a good deal of attention will be given to each person's *inner curriculum,* that is, one's sense of where he or she has been, is, and wants to be in the future. For too long this inner curriculum has been ignored to the detriment of leaders and those led. One of the greatest gifts adult educators can give children, as well as others, is to build on the memory of what it was like to be a child. In short, the creative curriculum leader must give attention to both political power and spiritual power. As M. Scott Peck has stated so eloquently, "political power is a matter of externals and spiritual power a matter of what is within" (Peck, 1993, p. 128). One must nurture the inner curriculum so that it serves as a foundation for outer curricula, and one must create outer curricula that enhance the inner curriculum. Both must be viewed as organic and growing, thus subject to change, rather than static and fixed.

As creative curriculum leaders we ask, "How can I understand myself better so that I enjoy my work and my life more?" and "How can I improve the settings (contexts) that are important to me?" Fortunately, there is no "right place" to begin our journey in answering these questions. The more I am meaningfully involved in activities within settings, the more I learn about myself and vice versa. The only serious mistake is hiding from self and not giving leadership to the creation of learning settings.

A caveat needs to be added as we begin our study of creative curriculum leadership. We don't have the resources to constantly be analytical. Although we need to consider preventive steps, we especially need to be aware of our culture and ourselves when things don't work out as they are supposed to, for it is precisely at this time that we need to know how our silent assumptions contribute to the problem (Schein, 1985).

In Part I, "The Meaning of Curriculum," Chapter 1 begins with a letter to the author from an educator in Charleston, South Carolina. The letter is provocative and poignant. She communicates the ways in which she has developed her own curriculum to integrate her professional and personal lives. In Chapter 2, "Defining Inner and Outer Curriculum," we search for a definition of curriculum that will help us reconcile the contradiction described in the introduction to this preface. The chapter leads us to the most common pitfall facing the educator involved in curriculum development—the view that development is a technical matter, with a set number of prescribed steps, rather than a creative artistic challenge. A related pitfall is the attitude that many involved in curriculum development have: "You should be where I am now." This attitude communicates the feeling that "I am above you and your problems and there is one right place to be in the curriculum development process." It belies the fact that development is a process in which each person unfolds gradually in order to grow and use a unique combination of talents and interests. And, the rescuer sometimes says, "You don't have to experience difficulties and pain like I did if you are where I'm at now." Yet, it is precisely from experiencing pain and difficulties that we learn and grow through self-discipline (Peck, 1978). It is the special responsibility of our schools "to provide the tools and to develop the skills through which the child can create his or her own experience" (Eisner, 1988, p. 15).

Part II, "Education as Vocation: How a 'Sense of Calling' Influences Curriculum Development," places self within the context of vocation. Vocation does not mean job or career but rather refers to the original meaning of the Latin verb *vocare*, "to call." What is it that "called" you to educational leadership? What is it that sustains you to continue giving educational leadership? What is the role of developing your own curriculum in relation to your answers to the two previous questions? Chapter 3, "Learning From Your Professional Autobiography," challenges you, the reader, to view self as instrumental in the curriculum leadership process (Combs, Avila, & Purkey, 1971). That is, curriculum leaders share with others (1) where they think they have been, (2) where they think they presently are, and (3) where they would like to be in the future. A number of self-appraisal inventories are used to face this challenge.

The interesting thing about being engaged in "know thyself" leadership activities is that you will hear and therefore discover more about yourself in front of others. This process of defining ourselves empowers us rather than letting others do this for us (Steinem, 1992). And empowerment of self is essential before significant changes or transformation can occur.

One of the main ways in which we empower ourselves and others is to enjoy the core of our work so much that we communicate this to others in our verbal and nonverbal actions. Chapter 4, "Looking Forward to Work: The Power of Wanting to Be There," treats this important matter by sharing in a student's own words how she knows if her teachers want to be with her. "Keeping the Fire in Your Vocation," the title of Chapter 5, suggests ways in which we can avoid or work our way out of burnout.

Part III, "Curriculum Development Can Make a Difference," presents concrete ways in which each of us can relate to self, others, and the environment as we develop curriculum. Chapter 6, "Creative Curriculum Leadership in Practice," defines such leadership as using our talents to help others identify and use their talents. Most definitions of leadership have a highly manipulative ring to them: "The secret is to get others to do what you want them to do whether they want to do it or not." Such definitions don't give members of a setting the feeling that they own the directions in which they are going. "Civility in Leadership: The Ultimate Difference," is the title of Chapter 7. This chapter presents the view that creative leaders set the stage by giving attention to civilities within the setting. Such civilities are an essential norm in the creation of curriculum within community (Peck, 1993). However, civilities are much more than manners and politeness. They must reflect the creative curriculum leader's basic character traits, such as honesty and integrity.

Readers will find cases (critical incidents) designed to stimulate thinking and discussion at the end of the chapters. The cases pick up on the problems and dilemmas in each chapter. In field-testing these cases, we have discovered that readers want to be actively involved in applying ideas from each chapter to settings in which they are leaders; cases are an excellent way to bridge theory and practice. You are asked to identify possible responses from which you choose a preferred response and rationale for it. Then compare and contrast your response and rationale to the author's preferred response and rationale. We have found in using these cases that they can stimulate educators to make informed decisions that can have a lasting effect on self and others.

You will see throughout this book that the creation of settings and community is a major theme and thesis. In fact, "community building is the ideal vehicle for the teaching of civility" (Peck, 1993, p. 284). And, it is in building community that we practice civility. The creative curriculum leader's motto could well be *"community building first, decision making second"* (Peck, 1993, p. 286). This is consistent with the definition of curriculum in the present book, *Creative Curriculum Leadership*: "What each person experiences as learning settings are cooperatively created."

Many educators were important in writing this book. Special appreciation is due to the leaders who field-tested the cases in seminars. *Intercultural Interactions*, by Richard W. Brislin, Kenneth Cushner, Craig Cherrie, and Mehealana Yong, was the model for the format used in identifying responses to cases. Thanks also goes to Scott, Foresman and Company for permission to use excerpts from the author's *Curriculum Planning: The Dynamics of Theory and Practice* (1982). Finally, Gracia A. Alkema, president of Corwin Press, Inc., is one of those rare editors who has resisted the lure of hierarchical relationship in favor of lateral "thinking out loud" conversations, and as a result, the author discovers new and exciting ways to share ideas and feelings with the reader. In short, Gracia lives creative leadership as it is described in this book—a gift to all of us.

E. Wayne Trogdon, superintendent of Asheville City Schools in Asheville, North Carolina, was helpful in sharpening my ideas on the role of evaluation in community building. He is the superintendent of schools featured in Chapter 2 of this book.

The format for this book is a creative one that invites your participation. In other words, the organization of the book has been selected to model for the reader what it is hoped the reader will in turn model for others. I would like to hear from you as to what you experienced in using the ideas in the book in your professional and personal lives. Please write to me at 232 Curry Hall, University of North Carolina at Greensboro, Greensboro, NC 27412. I promise a response.

About the Author

Dale L. Brubaker is a Professor of Education at the University of North Carolina at Greensboro. He was an assistant professor at the University of California, Santa Barbara, and an associate professor at the University of Wisconsin, Milwaukee. He is the author or co-author of 13 books, including *Teacher as Decision Maker, Creative Survival in Educational Bureaucracies,* and *Curriculum Planning: The Dynamics of Theory and Practice.* He received his Ph.D. in Education from Michigan State University.

PART I The Meaning of Curriculum

Activity in itself is not satisfying for any period of time. Meaning must be associated with our activity. For example, if you are given the assignment of moving sandbags from Place A to Place B and then from Place B to Place A simply to keep you busy, you will soon become bored with the task. If, on the other hand, you move sandbags from Place A to Place B (your front yard) to keep back floodwaters, you will indeed find meaning in the activity.

And so it is with developing curriculum as *a course of study*. This construction work must be meaningful to you, the builder, and the product you produce (the course of study) must also be a springboard that will stimulate personal meaning for those who use it.

The two major questions facing the creative curriculum leader, questions that link the inner curriculum (*what each person experiences as learning settings are cooperatively created*) and the outer curriculum (*the course of study*), are: "How shall I live with myself?" and "How shall we live with each other?" (Brubaker, 1989; Macdonald, 1977).

Chapter 1, "Introduction: Developing One's Own Curriculum," begins with an account of an educator's struggle to reconcile the inner curriculum and the outer curriculum. It is a creative curriculum leader's effort to locate authority in herself as well as in external forces.

Chapter 2, "Defining Inner and Outer Curriculum," discusses two definitions of curriculum, inner and outer, and the implications of

1

these definitions for the creative curriculum leader. It is argued that both definitions have their place, and we are challenged to create new and useful relationships between them.

The main goal of the two chapters is to catch you, the reader, up in the exciting activity of creative curriculum leadership.

1

Introduction:
Developing One's Own Curriculum

When we say that someone is a student, whether in the first grade or in high school, we tend to be more impressed with what they do not know and cannot do than with what they do know and are interested in.

Seymour B. Sarason (1993a, p. 190)

The title of this book, *Creative Curriculum Leadership*, as well as the immediate inspiration for writing it, came from a letter from Teri Gainey Bastian, an educator in Charleston, South Carolina. The letter, a sensitive and at times poignant account of her efforts to develop her own curriculum, bears quoting in its entirety, after which we will explore its meaning:

I want to share with you my observations for the past few years in the area of curriculum development. I decided to write you on the ride home with friends after your lecture on creative curriculum leadership so that I wouldn't forget anything. These ideas come from three primary areas: my career, my cousin, and my hobby.

Many of my colleagues and I bemoan the fact that the things we learned in our courses taken for the master's degree in education touch only a very small part of what we actually do on the job. What has been most helpful to us has been attending

3

conventions, talking to each other, attending workshops, and reading literature. In order to be really effective on our jobs we have needed far more information, experience, and stimulation than we had in our master's degree program.

At first I resented this fact. Then I realized that my cousin, who is a highly respected and nationally recognized CPA, has done something very similar within his vocation. He attends local, state, and national conventions. He reads leadership, management, and accounting literature constantly (even when he's grilling steaks). He participates on a national scale in peer review programs. *In short, he continuously is developing his own curriculum.*

As a hobby, I am an artist. Because I never drew anything but stick people until about 18 years ago, I decided to develop my own curriculum rather than entering a bachelor's degree program. I am an active member of three artist guilds. I attend workshops in areas of art that interest me. My entertainment budget goes to art books and magazine subscriptions. I also experiment with and "fail" at loads of art projects. I love not getting a grade from a teacher. Some people are very drawn to my work, but others are not. Mostly, though, I like it. I never took the first art course when I was in college because I was so fearful of not being "good at it." I know that a traditional art curriculum with a teacher "judging" my work would have ended my talent development. Instead, I love my art and actually sell quite a bit of it.

In being part of an innovative doctoral program, I have found a university that truly makes learning relevant to my work and life as a whole. I am constantly reminded of a poster of a giraffe that I had in my classroom with the inscription "Learning Is Life Long." I know that my life, no matter how long it lasts, will never be long enough to see and learn and do all the things I want.

Thanks for the invitation to write to you. This opportunity was a grand way to cope with the problem of the long ride home.

Sincerely,

Teri Gainey Bastian

P.S. I loved laughing and singing with you and my colleagues today. It was a once in a lifetime opportunity, but I wish it happened more. That's something I can do [something] about, isn't it?

The Letter's Meaning

Teri Gainey Bastian's words have the ring of truth because she writes from her experience in relating to universities and schools. In fact, the first thing we note is that curriculum as a course of study is an important but relatively minor part of her curriculum development. Another way to say this is that she places her own learning first. She sees herself at the center of learning rather than simply locating authority in external sources, such as textbooks and professors' lecture notes. She views her role as an actor who is motivated internally, rather than a reactor motivated externally. As Gloria Steinem says, "Self-authority is the single most radical idea there is and there is a real hunger for putting the personal and the external back together again" (Attinger, 1992, p. 55). The revolutionary nature of this thought is clear when one realizes that placing her own learning first runs counter to both the role of the student in university culture and the culture of the schools.

The higher the level of schooling the more the student is taught to devalue his or her own insights and value the insights of those whose ideas are considered to be more worthy. This may in part be because secondary schools are so much larger and more bureaucratized than earlier grades (Sarason, 1971). And high school teachers tend to emulate their best university professors, who are seen as purveyors of knowledge to be ingested by students. For example, imagine a doctoral student, who has selected a topic for a research paper or dissertation, beginning this quest by writing down all he or she knows on the subject. The very idea seems ludicrous, for we have all been advised to begin doing research by going to the library or doing a literature search on the views of others.

The K-8 educator is pressured in another direction. School buses and central office public relations officials advertise as follows: "Children First" and "Schools Are for Children." In short, high school and university classrooms place the student in the role of an empty vessel to be filled with ideas from external authorities, while

K-8 classrooms tend to define the teacher as a missionary minister-
ing to the lives of children. The effect of both cultures is to give the
educator a secondary learning role. At the same time, it is both
common sense and part of education folklore that a teacher or
administrator turned on to learning will probably create a climate
in which others are more likely to be turned on to learning. This is
simply one of the contradictions in education that can be detrimental to educators and students alike.

It is also true that problem solving, one of the major pedagogical
approaches in schools and universities, is based on a deficit model:
We focus on what is missing or wrong to the exclusion of what is
right and should be preserved. One of the reasons for this is that
problem-solving approaches begin with the question "What is the
problem?" rather than "How do I experience the problem?" For
example, the administrator or teacher usually senses the pain associated with a serious problem before framing the question "What is
the problem?" Educators often feel one or more of the following
maladies when a serious problem faces them: stomachaches, eating
too much, not being able to eat, headaches, inability to concentrate,
and waking up in a cold sweat. And yet, they are not asked to begin
the problem-solving process by sharing such personally important
experiences; rather, they are asked to immediately move to higher-
level thinking processes by focusing on questions such as "What is
the problem?" and "What alternative solutions are open to you?"
The removal of the student's experiences from Teri Gainey Bastian's
master's program courses is one of the reasons why "the courses
touch only a very small part of what we (master's students) do on
the job (as educators)."

Ralph Waldo Emerson stated the case for the primacy of experience in his "Essay on History," written in 1903:

> We are always coming up with the emphatic facts of history in
> our private experience and verifying them here. All history
> becomes subjective; in other words there is properly no his-
> tory, only biography. Every mind must know the whole lesson
> for itself—must go over the whole ground. What it does not
> see, what it does not live, it will not know. (p. 10)

Elliot Eisner confirms Emerson's thesis by stating, "it is the qualities we experience that provide the content through which meaning is secured" (Eisner, 1988, p. 16). The argument by both Emerson and Eisner for the primacy of experience is supported by Rollo May's statement that "thinking and self-creating are inseparable" (May, 1975, p. 116).

Because of an inadequate master's degree program, Teri, like her CPA cousin, adopted a very proactive stance and developed her own curriculum, consisting of "attending conventions, talking to each other, attending workshops, and reading literature." Furthermore, she continued to develop her own curriculum by using similar vehicles to become an artist—a hobby that stimulates her entire professional and personal life.

It is in "doing art" where Teri most dramatically follows her bliss. As a member of three artist guilds, she is part of support communities. She avoids the judgmentalism of grading by not taking courses where grades are assigned. In her own words, "I know a traditional art curriculum with a teacher 'judging' my work would have ended my talent development." Rather, she attends workshops that interest her and uses her entertainment budget to buy art books and magazine subscriptions. She recognizes that artistic expression leads to mixed reviews from critics. She has reconciled this contradiction by concluding "I love my art." In short, she has located authority in herself rather than in the judgments of others.

In locating authority in herself and her experiences, Teri yearns for and has achieved in large measure an integration of her learning. Such integration is challenged by a segmented view of curriculum in courses in high schools and universities. The position that each course's learning must be discrete was brought home to me during the final semester of my undergraduate education. During that year I experienced one of those rare moments when the learning from a variety of courses came together in a comprehensible and meaningful whole. European history, world drama, world literature, art appreciation, and world religions made sense to me in ways that were simply amazing. I sat down and wrote what I considered to be one of the best essay examination answers within my experience. The next day, the professor of the world religions class called and asked me to stop by his office for a conference. "I simply can't grade your exam," he said. Then he added, "I only wanted you to write what you had learned in this class." I left his office with a C+ for the most meaningful examination I had ever written. There is often a price for locating authority in self. One upsets the normal order of things, which can be painful to self and others. A letter from a college student to his mother illustrates this point:

> Dear Mom,
> I'm really enjoying college. Last week I learned how to ski for the first time and broke a leg. Thank heavens it wasn't mine.
> Love,
> Mike

It is important to make a distinction between the need for curriculum as a course of study and our evaluation of a particular course of study. Teri does not criticize the need for curriculum as a course of study, but she is wary of a traditional approach to curriculum because, in her view, it only locates authority outside the learner. Form, something that sets limits by excluding parts of objective reality, "provides the essential boundaries and structure for the creative act" (May, 1975, p. 140). George S. Counts, noted educator and colleague of John Dewey, said this in a humorous way: "The reason I want my children raised as Methodists is so that they have something to reject" (Brubaker, 1989). In other words, form and boundaries of the Methodist faith would give his children something to react to so that they could build their own faith. "Limiting and expanding thus go together" (May, 1975, p. 137). Discipline and creative imagination struggle in a kind of dialectic that must be reconciled by the creative curriculum leader. But without the conflict and struggle, there would be no exercise of human intelligence.

Conclusion

One of the reasons why Teri Gainey Bastian's letter is so powerful is that her ideas and feelings about curriculum development rest on a vision for learning that nurtures the curiosity all humans have from our earliest days (Sarason, 1993b). By assuming the leadership for her own learning, she develops her own curriculum. This doesn't discount curriculum as a course of study in schools and universities. It does, however, challenge us to define curriculum as a course of study in such a way that it is a springboard that releases our natural curiosity and our desire to "own" what is created. The next chapter speaks to the importance of defining curriculum.

Case 1: Choosing a Graduate School

After several years of experience as an educator, you feel ready to pursue graduate study. Your choice of graduate schools is between a traditional one and an innovative satellite program. Both are within an hour's driving distance and are credentialed by the state, so your economic benefits from completion of the degree are assured. You decide to attend recruitment and orientation sessions in the spring prior to your enrollment.

The speaker at the more traditional university summarizes the benefits as follows: (1) The program of study is established so that those who hire and promote you in your school system will be familiar with everything you do during graduate study; (2) there is a well-established library with excellent computer services; (3) professors don't come and go and can be counted on to see you through your program; (4) the curriculum (course of study) changes little from year to year, thus affording you security; and (4) administrators and professors have established networks to help you get jobs throughout the state.

The speaker for the satellite program is equally articulate and also summarizes the advantages of the innovative university: (1) You will be one of a group of pioneers whose enthusiasm and sense of community will be contagious; (2) computers will give you access to the information you need as a "scholar on your feet" so that you don't need a traditional library; (3) professors aren't tenured and you will get fresh ideas rather than hearing the same old ideas from the same professors; (4) your experiences in the work world will be part of the innovative curriculum; and (5) graduates from other satellite programs within the university will afford you access to a national network for employment opportunities.

Which university program will you enroll in for fall classes? Please choose the best response from the alternatives that follow:

1. Enroll in the traditional graduate program.
2. Enroll in the satellite graduate program.
3. Spend another semester or year investigating this matter.

Case 1: Rationales for the Alternative Responses

1. It is simply too risky to enroll in a nontraditional graduate program. Remember, pioneers are the ones who get arrows in their backs. You will benefit from the security and prestige of the traditional university, even though the economic benefits from the two university programs are identical. Graduates from the traditional university will support you when you graduate. After all, they have a vested interest in their own degree from the traditional university. Professors at the traditional university are a known quantity, and you can use your network of graduates to learn how to negotiate the degree program in an efficient way. If you opt for security over all else, the traditional university program is a good choice, but the tremendous changes in our society should prompt you to consider other choices.

2. It is hypocritical to talk about changes in our society and world as an educator while at the same time enrolling in a traditional program for reasons of security and prestige. The innovative program will give you an opportunity to build a bridge between your work world and the university. Since professors aren't tenured, the satellite university won't have to keep deadwood: You have to wake up some tenured professors to pay them. Since economic benefits and credentials are identical from the two universities, this is not a matter of concern. With regard to prestige, once you buy into pecking order thinking, there is no end to believing that this is better than that. Instead of focusing on what needs to be done, you give resources to trying to get and keep others' approval. It is important to remember that other graduates from satellite programs will have the enthusiasm of pioneers and will therefore actively help you find employment opportunities. To attend the innovative university program is a good choice.

3. Waiting a semester or year will give you a chance to gather more information. You will then have a stronger feeling about the rightness of your choice. The difficulty with this decision is that those who tend to put off a decision lose the benefits of taking the initiative. Being proactive and then keeping the momentum are the keys to successful completion of a graduate program. Get on with it. Therefore, consider a better choice.

2

Defining Inner and Outer Curriculum

Curriculum is the environment in the school and in the classroom. You have there in miniature what you have in life outside of the classroom and the school. Curriculum is therefore life! That's why it it is so vital and exciting. That's what makes it important. There's nothing out there that doesn't relate to curriculum.

James B. Macdonald (1977)

W e do not operate directly in reality but instead act on the basis of our maps (theories) of reality. According to Jürgen Habermas (1971), our major human interests are located in one of three places: control, understanding, or liberation. The primary orientation of each person's conception of curriculum planning, an essential part of creative curriculum leadership, is in one of these three places.

Conceptions of Curriculum Planning

If you are an educator, your first methods of teaching class imprinted in your mind the proper map for instruction and learning as well as the appropriate definition of curriculum. In fact, every teaching methods textbook used in teacher preparation classes has been organized according to this map or theory of pedagogical reality.

Think for a moment of the first lesson plan you ever wrote. You were taught to organize this lesson plan as follows: (1) select and behavioralize objectives; (2) select and organize activities (methods and materials) for student learning; and (3) evaluate the effectiveness of activities in reaching objectives (Tyler, 1949). This is referred to as the *Tyler rationale*. You were taught that there is a proper sequence to be followed in order to be a successful teacher. At a deeper level, you were assured you would not fail if you tried at all times to control the classroom environment in general and students in particular. If this sounds like a masculine, "take charge" rational approach, you have heard correctly (Lightfoot, 1983). Gloria Steinem (1992) speaks to this gender-related matter:

> I had been raised to assume all power was outside myself, but they [men] had been raised to place power almost nowhere but within themselves. Often, they were suffering too. Just as the fantasy of no control was the enemy of my self-esteem, the fantasy of total control was the enemy of theirs. (p. 22)

The technology of teaching rests on a scientific conception of pedagogy, the symbol of which is the number. "Counting outcomes and producing rates is synonymous with being rational" (Bogdan & Biklen, 1982, p. 116).

Curriculum leaders who are primarily interested in control speak in terms of an efficient educational system. A technically sound system, it is argued, will demonstrate progress in measurable terms. I am amazed and disquieted by the number of superintendents who use the terms *evaluation* and *measurement* synonymously, whereas, in fact, measurement is but one kind of evaluation or assessment. If our discussion of the control mode sounds like industrial or factory rhetoric, it is because this language originated in the early years of the Industrial Revolution. Alvin Toffler (1980), in his classic work, *The Third Wave*, describes how Second Wave civilization, industrial civilization, relies on measurement to prove that progress is inevitable (pp. 114-131). Thus, our allegiance to measurement is based on several myths that hold an industrial society together. To challenge such myths is to challenge those wedded to an industrial view of civilization.

The formula-driven Tyler rationale described above is obviously linear and sequential. This provides comfort, security, and the feeling of control. The curriculum planner knows what to do and in what order. Any curriculum planning challenge is a problem that can be solved with the proper organizational tools. The idea that some problems are dilemmas to be reconciled is foreign to the curriculum planner as controller. The efficiency expert must provide leadership in task-oriented settings. Followers in turn share the leader's (manager's) unquestioned faith that the setting can and should be controlled at all times. This implies that persons within such settings must be controlled and monitored in the interest of efficiency.

A curriculum leader, interested in implementing the control theory during the Management by Objectives (MBO) era, describes her enthusiasm for the movement:

> I was inwardly proud that I was asked to attend the conference, but I was anxious about the fact that my superintendent of schools would also attend. It was a 2-day conference on management by objectives. The curriculum conference leader introduced MBO by pointing out that Henri Fayol, a French industrialist, identified what he called management essentials in the year 1916. These essentials were planning, organization, command, coordination, and control. The conference leader informed the group that his experience with MBO proved its usefulness in any setting. He listed seven questions that the effective MBO leader should ask:
>
> 1. What needs to be done?
> 2. What are the best ways to do these things?
> 3. When must these things be done?
> 4. What resources will be needed?
> 5. What will constitute satisfactory performance?
> 6. How much progress will this lead to?
> 7. What changes will be needed to improve performance?

I was impressed with the simplicity and practicability of the MBO design. This design is one that will be supported by my staff for it will give them "something to get their teeth into" and they will see their progress. I also like the optimism in the plan. We can't go wrong.

While at the conference I had time to revise many of the charts distributed by the conference leader. I will use these charts to plot the progress of curriculum-leadership groups throughout the year.

Now that you have been introduced to the control orientation toward curriculum and curriculum planning, let us summarize criticisms of this approach:

1. Control is but one human interest and it is appropriate for non-human rather than human subjects (Macdonald, 1980, p. 2).

2. As with all technical approaches, attention is given to linear, sequential processes but not to basic assumptions below such processes.

3. This orientation fits the industrial view and this simply reinforces the status quo. It doesn't speak to the tremendous changes that have taken place in a postindustrial information age society. Information, for example, bombards people in simultaneous rather than linear, sequential ways.

Disenchantment with the limited scientific and technical dimensions of control theory has prompted some curriculum-planning leaders and scholars to give more attention to the humanities. Conceptual frameworks have been developed in order to stimulate interpretations and perspectives as alternatives to the 1949 Tyler rationale.

The methodology of hermeneutics (understanding) has led many scholars to reject much of the scientific-technical language of control theorists in favor of less restrictive ways of conversing about curriculum and curriculum planning (Brubaker, 1989; Macdonald, 1980). One of the reasons for these conversations is that our experience tells us that we usually learn more as educators when things are somewhat out of control. That is, we are challenged by surprises in spite of the fact that we try to avoid such surprises. Patrick Welsh (1987), author of *Tales out of School*, describes this matter: "The books on pedagogy stress the importance of control in the classroom. But it's often when things are a little out of control—when I get a queasy feeling in my stomach—that real learning takes place." This dilemma is continually brought to my attention as I talk to superintendents of schools about their relationships with school boards. "Why is it that you have such a good relationship with your board?" I ask. "We had an agreement from the beginning that there would be no surprises," they respond. "When do you learn the most?" I then ask. "When there are surprises," they answer. The superintendent's roles as politician and learner are often contradictory.

A major result of the scholarship of many hermeneutic thinkers is emphasis on the student (including the student of curriculum planning) as a creator, not just a consumer, of curriculum. Maxine Greene (1975), for example, writes about the networks of relationships that all curriculum planners create. The idea of networking (network creating) sees the person as having internal authority to informally stretch in many and diverse directions that are not predetermined. As a result, the networker increases his or her sense of efficacy.

What are the practical implications of hermeneutic theory for curriculum leadership and planning? The following description of a curriculum project will help us answer this question.

> John was clear as to his goals for involvement in the Stone Street Project at the onset. These goals fit with the project goals: (1) to systematically build a knowledge base focusing on bureaucratic and professional forces exerted on decision makers in all similar organizations; (2) to weigh the extent to which decision makers can and should operate in the professional decision-making mode in the area of curriculum and instruction, while at the same time operating most effectively in the bureaucratic mode in noncurriculum and instruction (governance) matters; and (3) to disseminate findings, with special attention given to what might and might not be useful to other leaders in similar settings.

John felt that these understandings might lead to strategies for change in the setting being studied, but this wasn't his main interest. In fact, in his own mind, John thought that understandings achieved might well lead to the development of strategies for change that would be initiated in another setting at another time.

Those who advocate understanding as a primary interest of curriculum planners have been criticized in many different ways including the following:

1. Philosophical analysis and criticism can lead to understanding but equal attention should be given to the implementation of such understanding in settings. Hermeneutics theory stands back and tries to objectify too much (Macdonald, 1980, p. 5).

2. It is not in step with our culture's scientific and technical way of viewing things. It is therefore of little practical use. Since most of our society's organizations are highly bureaucratic, hermeneutic theory simply doesn't prepare persons for their roles in such organizations.

The third conception of curriculum leadership and planning is based on the assumption that *praxis* (reflective action) has the potential "for emancipating human beings from unnecessary social constraints on their freedom" (Macdonald, 1980, p. 5). Curriculum planners who are primarily interested in liberation give attention to "the forming of social relations, rewards, and learning expectations in curriculum by economic and occupational interest structures, social class and power structure, and the use of language as distorted by work and power arrangements, as well as the form of language itself" (Macdonald, 1980, p. 6).

Critical theorists of this persuasion recognize the role that control and understanding must play in curriculum planning, but they want to go a third step. It is their emphasis on self-reflection through praxis that bonds these scholars together.

What is it that the curriculum planner must do? The curriculum planner must (1) identify and understand ways in which persons are dominated or constrained, (2) know what potentialities can be emancipated or liberated, and (3) guide progressive social development (Macdonald, 1980).

The following case illustrates a curriculum planner engaged in the liberation frame of mind:

> Jamie was a student of her culture and society as well as a student of other cultures and societies. She was especially concerned that our society has given a good deal of attention to the psychology of the person but little attention to the psychology of organizations. She saw her role as a curriculum planner as including giving attention to this societal reality.
>
> When Jamie entered into the alliance with other curriculum leaders, she wanted to know if they shared her concern for the psychology of organizations. Most did, which was enough to spur Jamie on in the project. As the curriculum-planning group began to get the project off the ground, Jamie reminded them that changes aimed at the person were misdirected, for a changed person could reenter an organization and be absorbed or co-opted by the organization itself. She therefore argued that the curriculum leadership team should give most of its attention to making organizational changes from which personal changes would evolve. For example, she felt that there should always be at least two educators from a school system in attendance at conferences and meetings. In this way they would have a support group in their home school settings.
>
> At the same time, Jamie emphasized the role of self-reflection on the part of persons, especially the core group of leaders in the project.

Criticism of the liberation point of view has come from many quarters. The following is a summary of some of this criticism.

1. Bureaucratic structures in our society simply will not tolerate moving beyond understanding to action. The fabric of our society will not take the pushing and shoving that we endured in the 1960s.

2. We are so locked into technical processes in our society that liberation processes will not fit. The person who practices liberation and emancipation will surely be a social misfit.

3. Few leaders are capable of integrating theory and practice. Praxis, reflective action, is an ideal that is too demanding in the real world.

In this section of the chapter, it has been demonstrated that the curriculum leader's conception of curriculum planning influences his or her curriculum-planning behaviors. Both behaviors and conceptions are based on a foundation or substructure we identified as basic assumptions.

The Outer Curriculum and the Inner Curriculum

The control orientation of the curriculum leader, in the culture of curriculum as a course of study, rests on the assumption that authority is located outside the learner (student and teacher) in textbooks, curriculum guides, and courses of study. This is why we refer to it as the *outer curriculum*. Transmission of knowledge, part of the mimetic tradition, is the goal (Jackson, 1986). (The Greek word *mimetes* means "imitator.") The key question raised by followers of the mimetic tradition is: "What knowledge is of most worth?"

Since authority is located in textbooks, curriculum guides, and the like, teachers can easily assign blame to someone above them in the hierarchy: "They wrote a poor textbook." "The curriculum guide is inadequate." "The principal told me I had to do it this way." Teachers know that authority for the curriculum is located in administrators' interpretations of written materials, but teachers often misinterpret and sometimes don't even know the content of written materials. For example, teachers in a leadership seminar were asked if a sense of mission was important in their school system. A participant excitedly raised her hand. "We had a nationally known consultant work with us on a mission statement." "What is your mission?" she was asked. "I don't know," she replied. "It's back at my school in a notebook."

There is a hierarchy of subject matter in the culture of curriculum as a course of study. Some courses' grades don't count when colleges and universities compute a prospective student's grade-point average. In effect, band, orchestra, dance, art, and some other subjects are considered *extra*curricular. This fits with the age-old conception that people who work with their hands don't use their heads. The "some animals are more equal than others" philosophy is also expressed when students who take advanced "academic" subjects receive bonus points that increase their grade-point averages.

The culture of curriculum as a course of study has a left-brain orientation; the self is seen as a subset of the world (Bogen, 1979). The learner's experiences take a backseat to external authorities. Curriculum as a course of study is always reactive, never proactive. You will read about future curriculum topics in the editorial pages of newspapers. In short, teachers are curriculum implementors (reactors) not curriculum makers (actors). Infantilization of schools, schooling, and teachers can result from the bureaucratization of curriculum as a course of study. Teachers are treated like children rather than professionals.

The culture of the *inner curriculum*, "what each person experiences as learning settings are cooperatively created," has a very different orientation. Consider briefly what these people have in common:

- A custodian with a special interest in wildflowers leads a middle-school class on a nature-trail walk, with the teacher at the end of the line of students.
- An assistant principal in a high school makes a point of being in the company of a student who was disciplined the previous day, so that the student will continue to feel accepted.
- An elementary school principal eats breakfast once a week with bus drivers and emphasizes their special role in reaching children.
- A teacher engaged in lunchroom supervision teaches socially unschooled children table manners.

The teachers and principals in these situations believe that curriculum as a course of study is simply a springboard for inner curriculum, "what each person experiences as learning settings are cooperatively created" (Brubaker, 1982). (Imagine the outer curriculum as a rectangle inside of inner curriculum in the shape of an amoeba. Curriculum as a course of study is something to react to as persons grow, learn, and change.)

The primary role of experience in the inner curriculum places this way of viewing teaching and learning in the ontological realm. That is, one's being (who one is) is more important than what one does (Tillich, 1952). (The person's inner thoughts, basic assumptions about reality, and intentions will not always be visible in one's behavior.) As stated in the introduction to Part I, "The Meaning of Curriculum," a major question raised by those interested in the inner curriculum is "How shall I live with myself?" The challenge is to be autobiographical without being narcissistic. A second major question is "How shall we live together?" Interaction between the self and others in community is a natural area of study for the curriculum scholar.

The inner curriculum rests firmly in the transformative rather than the mimetic tradition (Jackson, 1986). The teacher and students are learners who are expected to experience "a qualitative change often of dramatic proportion, a metamorphosis, so to speak" (Jackson, 1986, pp. 120-121). As Jackson has clearly stated, authority is located in the person's search for understanding and liberation; and as a result of this search, something within the learner, his or her essence, changes (Jackson, 1986).

The masculine effort to take charge and to control what we found in the tradition of curriculum as a course of study now incorporates the feminine intuitive, artistic role. There is an element of control within understanding and liberation, but control is clearly not the dominant interest of the person oriented to the culture of the inner curriculum (Habermas, 1971).

Those who commit themselves to the inner curriculum make themselves vulnerable in ways that outer curriculum advocates do not. Contradictions, paradoxes, and dilemmas are grist for the inner curriculum person's inquiry. Single causation is replaced by multiple causation and, at times, no known causation. Mystery can play an important heuristic role. Chance and serendipity are often entertained as part of the artists' common bond—an interest in quality rather than quantity. (Can you imagine a case being made that Renoir was a better painter than another artist because his canvases were larger or that he painted more of them?)

The educator with an inner curriculum orientation knows that the setting of ends, activity selection, and evaluation are often simultaneous processes rather than part of a linear, sequential formula. Goals, intentions of a general nature, open up new vistas for exploration. Behavioral objectives too often constrict the learner, thereby treating him or her as a passive vessel rather than as an active learner. Goal-free evaluation can play an important role since it stimulates the learner's involvement in creative activities without constricting him or her to predetermined ends.

Because authority is located in the learner's search for understanding and liberation, he or she is responsible for decisions made during the search. Collegiality, rather than hierarchical command-down decision making, means that the educator oriented to the inner curriculum can't blame higher-ups for difficulties in the system. And advocates of the inner curriculum are encouraged to be proactive rather than simply reactive. Inner curriculum is lived. Outer curriculum is taken. We create each other and ourselves in the formation of community as advocates of the inner curriculum.

The culture of the inner curriculum is primarily right-brain oriented, with the world seen as a subset of the self (Bogen, 1979). Or, as Emerson said, "Every mind must know the whole lesson for itself" (1903, p. 10). A superintendent of schools, who is committed to the inner curriculum, describes the difference this view of curriculum made in his leadership:

> Two themes are central to me as a superintendent of schools: empowerment and the improvement of services. The traditional top-down compliance system approach to leadership simply doesn't work. It takes too much time to micromanage people, and this way of doing things denies people ownership. People sit around waiting for the next order and can always blame someone higher up, rather than accepting responsibility for their work. Our greatest asset is the minds and souls of adults expected to give services to students. When they feel they have authority over the work they do, the result is greater self-understanding, productivity, and higher morale. The inside-out definition of the inner curriculum helps each person find authority in himself or herself and emphasizes cooperation and teamwork as we create learning environments for all interested in schools—children and adults.

One example illustrates what I've done to support the inner curriculum of principals. I inherited a checklist system for evaluating principals. I continued to use the checklist for a couple of years because principals were used to it, but I added a section that was a handwritten profile of each principal's leadership. Principals were also asked for their own self-portrait of their leadership. The sharing of these subjective accounts is all that counts now with the principals. We've simply eliminated the checklists.

What the superintendent of schools has done in reality is to invite principals and others to be human and authentic.

Conclusion

Curriculum as a course of study, and curriculum as what each person experiences as learning settings are cooperatively created, are human inventions (definitions) that serve as a major tool by which one creates environments that later shape and influence one's own behavior (Yinger, 1978). In effect, each definition is persuasive and evaluative, for it is an attempt to alter attitudes in a desired direction. This is the challenge facing curriculum leaders, one that we should all find an invitation to learning and action. In the next section of this book we will see how one's vocation or "calling" influences his or her desire to be with students and colleagues. And, we will treat the important matter of continuing to want to be there, or avoiding burnout.

Case 2: You Are Asked for Your Definition of Curriculum at a Staff Development Retreat

You are a member of the Site-Based Management Curriculum Council in your school. This five-member group, consisting of three teachers, a parent, and the assistant principal, has planned an excellent conference (retreat) for faculty and five parents who represent the community. You look forward to the dialogue, good fellowship, food, and recreation.

The opening session consists of a guest speaker from the university, after which there will be five "breakout" groups that will react to the speaker's address. You and the other members of the curriculum council will give leadership to the breakout groups.

The speaker challenges the audience to define curriculum as what each person experiences as learning settings are cooperatively created, rather than simply as a course of study. The speaker adds that curriculum as a course of study should be the best it can be, but it is ultimately only a springboard for all of the learning experiences students and teachers acquire.

As the head of one of the five discussion groups, it is your responsibility to begin the discussion by giving your reaction to the speaker. What will you say? Please choose the best response from the alternatives that follow:

1. Disagree with the speaker. Curriculum has traditionally been defined as a course of study, and you believe that this is both necessary and sufficient.
2. Agree with the speaker. Support this innovative definition.
3. State the position that the definition of curriculum is of little consequence.

Case 2: Rationales for the Alternative Responses

1. The speaker's message is very troublesome. It provides each teacher the license to go in any direction he or she pleases. It ignores or minimizes the fact that there is an essential body of knowledge that must be learned by all students. State your case passionately and warn members of the group of impending chaos if the innovative definition of curriculum is adopted. The difficulty in this response is that it immediately locks you into the traditional without considering alternative responses. Please consider other possible reactions.

2. The speaker has delivered a powerful and important message. Each person's experiences are central to curriculum. This definition includes students and teachers. Curriculum is indeed a springboard

that must be revised to meet new societal and school needs. This is a good choice; lead the discussion in your group to the application of the innovative definition of curriculum to school settings. The curriculum council will have an important role to play in reviewing and revising curriculum as a course of study. The principal and assistant principal will need to understand that they are catalysts and coordinators rather than directors.

3. One's definition of curriculum is of little consequence compared to one's actions as a curriculum leader. Theory is a smokescreen that takes educators' attention away from practice. Although there is some truth in this argument, one's definition of curriculum can be a map for creative curriculum leaders. Leaders who deny the value of defining curriculum may well be viewed as cynics. At the very least, they lose the opportunity to establish an affinity connection with those who want an operating definition of curriculum. Choose a better response.

Case 3: PTA Speaker Endorses National Curriculum Standards

The president of your school's Parent Teacher Association is a professor from a nearby university. The PTA president has invited a nationally recognized education expert to speak at the fall meeting. You are invited to respond to the speaker's address because of your leadership and speaking ability.

A large turnout is present for the address, and the speaker delivers a dynamic and often humorous lecture. She argues that national education policy has been set for the next 4 to 8 years, and at the head of the list is the need for national education standards, national curriculum frameworks, and a national examination system. She adds that the national examinations will tell us how curriculum is operationally defined. Evaluation of students will include performance assessment, projects, and portfolios. The speaker concludes by saying that we will have to live with a paradox: a national orientation to education that is local in implementation. And teachers must serve as coaches who will help students beat Educational Testing Service in much the same way that Advanced Placement teachers presently try to beat the test makers. Teachers who are up to it will be inventive brokers who relate to the national-local paradox. Such teachers will do extraordinary work to reach and surpass national standards. Competition will be the driving force that will elicit the best in teachers and students. When the system is working correctly, it will look much like architectural competition. All competitors must meet building codes, but creativity will bloom.

It is now time for your reaction to the speech. What will you say? Please choose the best response from the alternatives that follow:

1. The price for following the speaker's advice is simply too high. State your case for this position.
2. The speaker is on target. Support the speaker's position with all of the expertise you have.
3. This is a non-issue. Explain why.

Case 3: Rationales for the Alternative Responses

1. The idea of a national curriculum with a national examination system is a serious mistake. Each student is unique and should be challenged to use his or her talents to the best of his or her ability. The speaker's position, if implemented, would sort students into winners and losers. It is an antidemocratic position. In fact, the national testing and curriculum movement creates large bureaucracies that further inhibit teachers, thus sapping their creativity.

2. The speaker is on target. We must have high expectations for all children. We have made education so unresponsive to the individual that we have neglected standards. In fact, the speaker's position is very democratic because it is a pathway to equal opportunity for all who work hard. Therefore, a democracy based on merit can finally be achieved in our country. All children will benefit. Furthermore, competition is at the very heart of our social structure. Students need to learn to compete in order to survive in our culture. In relating to this position favorable to the speaker's thesis, the educator must simply ask if the benefits outweigh the costs. My position is that they don't and the cost is primarily focused on the teacher's professional judgment and creativity. In fact, many bureaucratic measures designed to eliminate teachers who are considered to

be "bad apples" fail to rid the profession of incompetents, while at the same time curtailing the creative efforts of exemplary teachers.

3. It certainly gets one's attention to say that this is a non-issue. The difficulty is that the issue simply won't go away by calling it a non-issue. The movement toward national testing and curriculum is very much with us today.

PART II Education as Vocation: How a "Sense of Calling" Influences Curriculum Development

In Part I, "The Meaning of Curriculum," we saw that the inner curriculum (what each person experiences as learning settings are cooperatively created) and the outer curriculum (course of study) are interactive and interdependent. In Part II, we will give attention to the creative curriculum leader's view of vocation. We commonly think of one's vocation as his or her job or career, but the Latin verb *vocare*, "to call," has a much deeper and comprehensive meaning—particularly with respect to those who enter the field of education.

Some educators have had a "sense of destiny" with regard to teaching from the time they were little children (Peck, 1993). An educator in the Midwest talks about her sense of destiny:

> My kindergarten teacher and I had the same last name, and so when I played school in the neighborhood, I was usually chosen to be the teacher. After school and during the summertime, my friends and I went to the playground and I was usually "the teacher" during recess time. I knew that I wanted to be a teacher from the time I was 5. In fact, I wanted to be one of the best, just like my best teachers.

An interesting thing about the feeling that you are called to do great things is that your "calling will likely be worked out in ways that you currently can't even begin to imagine" (Peck, 1993, p. 70). The Midwestern educator continues her story:

My career path is a real mystery to me. After teaching for 10 years, I became interested in special education because of a special child in my classroom whom I didn't think I was reaching. I returned to school, got my master's degree in special education, and became a special education teacher. Then I was asked to become director of special education in the school system. This led me to a doctoral program with a major in special education. A year ago, a friend at the university started a special education program for preschool children and asked me to follow her as the director of the program. I had no idea at age 5 that I would be involved in so many different things, but I still have the same love for children that I had when I was a child.

It is with regard to the educator's love for children and desire to be helpful that participants in creative curriculum leadership seminars have had the most provocative discussions. One participant commented: "The bottom line for me as an educator is that I have always wanted to be helpful. In fact, in talking to my friends, we have agreed that we often play the martyr role." She continued, "In what other profession do you want to go to the bathroom but can't? I developed the martyr role so well that at times I felt that I shouldn't get anything out of teaching. I asked myself, 'Why?' I finally concluded that when I don't play the martyr role, I show my vulnerability and others have a string to pull. They can control me and, more than anything else, I wanted to control others as a helpful rescuer."

A special education teacher added, "There is a whole new world out there for exceptional children now, and I want to give children the same rights as other children have. My challenge is to be an advocate who cares rather than a caretaker who does for, rather than with, special children."

A third educator said, "I not only wanted to control students by being a rescuer but I wanted to fix their problems quickly. In the process, I thought things were my problems that weren't."

A colleague in school administration introduced another dimension to the discussion: "I had my own vision as to what education should be and discovered as a teacher I had little power. I moved into administration to get that power and do good things for children." She added, "One thing that motivated me to move into administration was that I didn't like what most school administrators did with power."

A seminar participant captured the *zeitgeist* ("feeling in the air") of our discussion: "You know, you really have to have your head on straight in relating to your vocation."

In Chapter 3, "Learning From Your Professional Autobiography," we will discuss those influences that have shaped your sense of calling, or vocation. The talents you have developed were probably sharpened by comments from parents, teachers, scout leaders, coaches, friends, and others in the community. We will explore these comments and the decisions you have made with regard to them. In some cases you have accepted such influences, whereas in other cases you have decided to move in new directions.

Chapter 4, "Looking Forward to Work: The Power of Wanting to Be There," discusses a source of power available to you that has received little attention in education literature—your desire to do what you do at work. Nobody always wants to go to work or always likes work, but if you consistently enjoy the core of your work, there is a much greater chance that you will be successful at what you do.

Chapter 5, "Keeping the Fire in Your Vocation," focuses on how experienced educators fight burnout and boredom. They have learned to find ways in which they can continue to be motivated to be creative curriculum leaders.

We will see in this section of the book that each person is both unique and precious. And "we have it within our power to change our nature when we need to" (Peck, 1993, p. 82). Another way to say this is that each of us writes his or her life script.

It should be added that creative curriculum leaders exist within particular cultures of organizations, and these cultures may vary considerably (Peck, 1993). We are therefore confronted with the question, "How do we decide what kind of culture we are called to?" (Peck, 1993, p. 238). This question speaks to one's comfort and vision with regard to where power is located and how it is exercised. This matter will be addressed in the chapters that follow.

3

Learning From Your Professional Autobiography

Each of us has an inner child of the past living within us. Those who needed to build no walls have access to that child's creativity and spontaneity. Those who had to leave this crucial core behind can tear down the walls, see what the child needed but didn't have, and begin to provide it now.

Gloria Steinem (1992, pp. 38-39)

Your sense of calling, or vocation, is an inner voice that gives you direction in your educational profession and indeed in life itself. Before we look at those factors that have shaped your life and vocation, let us examine those vital forces that may serve you in doing autobiography.

The first force that helps involve us in telling our story and being a creative curriculum leader is recognizing that *one is always a choice maker*. Some contemporary psychiatrists and psychologists have made an important contribution in helping us see that we are not victims of others' decisions. Rather, we always have the power to make decisions that influence ourselves, others, and the environment. Let us examine an extreme case to illustrate the power we always have as choice makers. Imagine for a moment that my bureaucratic superior is dissatisfied with my work and therefore decides to fire me. If I were in the victim frame of mind, I might well tell you, "My boss fired me," after which I would say things to get

33

your support and sympathy for me as a victim of another person's whims. I might also say that the situation in which I worked was impossible and I just couldn't do anything about it. If, on the other hand, I recognize that I always have the power to make decisions, I might say to you, "My boss fired me and I've decided to respond to this by doing thus and so." In this latter case I wouldn't play innocent by pretending that I have no power to respond to the boss's action (May, 1972). There is a world of difference between these two frames of mind and this difference can be seen in the attitudes and behaviors of educators. The following expressions and phrases reflect differences between the "victim" and the "nonvictim":

Victim	Nonvictim
"I can't do anything as long as this person is boss."	"I can't do everything I want to do while this person is boss, but I can do some things that are important to me."
"Nothing I do will make a difference."	"I can make a difference."
"What's the use?"	"What I do is important."

The nonvictim way of thinking is not meant to discount the very real pain and suffering that occur in the world today. Nor is it meant as a rationale for not helping those who are in trouble. It does say that those in dire straits cannot begin to help themselves out of such difficulty until they realize that they are choice makers.

The view that a person always has choices has a rich tradition in literature. John Steinbeck uses this view as the theme and thesis for *East of Eden* (1952). Lee, the Chinese servant of Adam Trask, shares with Adam the secret that he has spent 10 years trying to understand a brief part of the Cain and Abel story in Genesis. It is the part where Jehovah asks Cain why he is so angry. Jehovah says, "If thou doest well, shalt thou not be accepted? and if thou doest not well, sin lieth at the door. And unto thee shall be his desire, and *thou shalt* rule over him" (emphasis added). It was the *thou shalt* part that troubled Lee, for it was God's promise that Cain could conquer sin. For 2 years Lee went to nearby San Francisco to study with learned Chinese scholars about this passage in Genesis. These scholars invited a learned rabbi to study with them. Together they discovered that the Hebrew word *timshel* should be interpreted "thou mayest," which also led them to the conclusion that "thou mayest not." Lee discovered that *persons always have a choice.*

A second force that gives vitality to the creative curriculum leader and autobiographer is *intentionality*. Paul Tillich (1952), noted theologian and philosopher, argued that "man's vitality is as great as his intentionality" (pp. 81-82). Our intentions naturally flow from our sense of efficacy: "I can make a difference" becomes "I will make a difference by doing thus and so."

A third force evolves from a *sense of efficacy and intentionality*. It is the power of a dream of what is desirable and possible to accomplish. Knowing that I can make a difference, and intending to do good things, must be followed by a dream or vision of what is desirable and possible to accomplish. This dream is often painted with broad brush strokes rather than fine, detailed lines. The dream begins with "I wonder if. . . . " (See Chapter 6, "Creative Curriculum Leadership in Practice," for a more detailed discussion of personal and organizational vision.)

What Can I Learn From My Professional Autobiography?

The challenge is to think through and then express the patterns and principles that have been operative in one's educational experience (Pinar, 1975). In the process, the creative curriculum leader as autobiographer will achieve a deeper self-understanding generally. In listening to others relate their professional autobiographies, he or she will begin to arrive at an understanding of patterns of influences on decision makers, as realized in their behavior (Pinar, 1975). The special benefit to women and persons in other marginalized groups is cited by Gloria Steinem (1992): "I combined this research [on the factors that affect self-esteem] with women's personal stories, which are, like all personal accounts of any group that has been marginalized, our best textbooks: the only way to make our experience central" (p. 4).

Where do curriculum leaders start in order to use their autobiographies to make sense of their professional decision-making styles? William Pinar, curriculum theorist, suggests that we begin with free-flowing associative forms of thinking. The following serves as an example:

> I really enjoy trying to make sense out of what goes on in schools and I try to do this in a systematic way. . . . Where did I get this interest? My father was a fantastic bridge player and worker of crossword puzzles. . . . I think this helped me respect the mind and the exercise of intelligence. . . . I have a real concern for the person as a learner and I am interested in the social forces that influence the person. . . . Where does this come from? . . . I grew up in a small town in Wisconsin which gave me a sense of community. . . . The fact that this town was located in Wisconsin's liberal atmosphere was also a factor. . . . And, my mother had a real moral sense in that she believed that some things were ethically just and good. She dinged away at that. . . . (Macdonald, 1977)

Critical incidents in one's life, often related to one's professional life, can precipitate hard psychological work. One good way to do this work is by writing a story of what happened to you and the sense you made of this critical incident. You may or may not wish to share your writing with a trusted friend. The following educator's story illustrates story writing:

> A few days ago I woke up in a cold sweat. "What is the problem?" I said to myself and then to my wife. After brainstorming a bit, it was clear that I dreaded going to a meeting largely because I was going to be the only person of my gender there. Why did this bother me? The committee was charged with hearing the grievance of a faculty member against the department chair. Both were also of the other, rather than my, gender. Why was this gender issue important to me? Discussion with my wife helped me see that I placed myself in the rescuer role. I hated hearing the voice of judgment I associated with my father, the voice I was charged with invoking as a

committee member, and my way of coping with voice of judgment was the same one I acted out as a child: I tried to rescue my mother from my father. I felt intense pressure to rescue the "aggrieved" woman faculty member from the voice of judgment. I had identified the silent assumption underlying my stress. This understanding lifted the dark cloud overhead and I went to the meeting and played the role of another committee member rather than the rescuer.

Curriculum students often find it difficult to construct professional autobiographies. They have said things like: "We aren't used to giving our opinions since our teachers, especially in college, always wanted us to be objective." "This seems so subjective." "Our professors taught us to be scientific, and this doesn't seem very scientific." Always locating power in others can make one empathysick. Gloria Steinem (1992) describes how this happened to her:

> I finally began to admit that I, too, was more aware of other people's feelings than my own; that I had been repeating the patterns of my childhood without recognizing them . . . and in short, my childhood years—a part of my life I thought I had walled off—were still shaping the present as surely as a concealed magnet shapes metal dust. (p. 7)

Proponents of the autobiographical method recognize the rich source of ideas and feelings within each of us. Furthermore, the many and diverse ways of looking at life around us are a reality to those who hold them. A simple example will illustrate how perceptions of an event, the opening of summer school in a university, vary:

> In walking to my office at the university today, 2 weeks prior to the official opening of summer school, I stopped to talk to the men who were putting asphalt on the student parking lot. One man remarked, "We won't be able to start summer school on time since the parking lot won't be ready." A similar attitude prevailed at the bookstore, where the aisles were filled with boxes of books ready to be opened and shelved. A clerk said, "We've never been so far behind." Workers in the central administration

building had a different view as they registered students and collected tuition money with the knowledge that summer school would indeed start on time.

Participants in the creative curriculum leadership process can simply be expected to have differing perceptions of events. These perceptions are formed in part by their personal histories, which is basically the argument for giving attention to such autobiographies. As we participate in the process of sharing autobiographies, we begin to attain a *reciprocity of perspectives*. Out of our subjective perspectives emerge rationality and meaning, for perspectives blend and perceptions confirm each other.

Beginning to Do an Autobiography

As you complete the following talent inventory, you will flesh out a portrait of your calling, or vocation. During a typical day at work, you will use more talents than you probably realize you have. Your first task is to write in the left column a chronology of an ideal (best) school-year day. Please do this from the time you get up in the morning until the time you go to sleep at night. The first item or two may read something like this: 6 a.m. got up; 6:15 a.m. showered and put on favorite clothes; 6:30 ate a good breakfast; and so on. Your second task is to list in the second column the unique qualities (talents) you used in correspondence with the times you listed in the first column. Each of these qualities is a "tape" that goes off in your head when you encounter a particular situation. For example, 8:15 a.m. "I used my organizational skills to introduce a new lesson." Your third task is to name, in the third column, the sources of the tape you listed in the second column. These sources may include a parent or parents, a teacher, a religious figure, an aunt, an uncle, a grandparent, a friend, or others. For example, 9 a.m. "I took the students to the media center and introduced them to basic computer skills for finding materials. My aunt, an alumnus of the college I attended, introduced me to the college by taking me to its library. I've loved libraries and media centers ever since."

Your final task is to write in the fourth column your decision to either keep and act out the tape from childhood, or reverse the tape and not act it out as you were instructed to as a child. For example, 2 p.m. "I used my intelligence and physical bearing to break up a fight at school." "The tape that went off in my head was to get away from the fight. That's what my parents, teachers, and other adults taught me. But I then reversed the tape, because I knew that in my role as teacher, I had to address the matter rather than walk away from it."

Hundreds of educators have responded to this talent inventory. Some of the talents they have listed are preparation skills; organizational skills; proactivity; follow-through; the ability to be articulate, verbally and in writing; a sense of humor; the ability to motivate others to work together on committees; being a good team member; and being firm but fair with students.

One of the main findings of educators in completing the talent inventory is the seemingly endless array of contradictions that face them (Brubaker & Simon, 1993). That is, they are expected to somehow reconcile opposing or mixed messages. After reading the following list of contradictions, educators were asked to create metaphors that describe best their reactions to the list. They responded, "I sometimes feel like I'm herding cats." "I feel like a juggler." "It's like steering a dog by moving its tail." The somewhat general contradictions they listed were:

Professional autonomy but state regulation and supervision;

Told that we are professionals with expertise but outside consultants are the experts;

Competition with other schools but cooperation with other schools expected;

Display accomplishments but quietly go about your business;

Think (plan) ahead but catch up (look backward);

And be positive but face the negative.

It is clear from educators' responses to this exercise that contradictions are double-edged. They are often a source of consternation while at the same time a challenge that can bring out our creativity

A TALENT INVENTORY

Chronology of an Ideal (Best) School--Year--Day	My Unique Qualities In This Day (Tapes)	Sources of These Tapes	Personal Decisions to Keep These Tapes (Act on Them)

Purpose Statement: My purpose is to use my talents of _____, and _____ to support and inspire others to identify and use their talents.

CREATIVE LEADERSHIP USING TALENT PLAN

as educators. How is this possible? Contradictions produce interior tension that awakens us from comfortable routines, traditions, and rituals. "There is a constant battle in each of us," according to psychiatrist Arnold A. Hutschnecker (1974), "between the forces of excitation and inhibition" (p. 8). And it is the contradictions that really bother us that force us to be proactive as creative curriculum leaders. There is always an element of anxiety in this proactivity. The role of anxiety in creativity has been recognized by artists throughout the ages. Michelangelo's paintings of human beings have distended or dilated eyes, a telltale sign of anxiety (May, 1975).

Some contradictions call for hard psychological work. Others are a cause for celebration, even though they also require different kinds of work—usually of a more technical, logistical nature. For example, Janet and Jim are very bright students who recently joined your class. You enjoy their creative insights, but they are so quick that you find it hard work to create challenging assignments for them while other students plod along. The payoff for you is that you learn more as a teacher because of this challenge and so do other students in the class.

Or, take the instance of a principal in a large middle school. Two faculty members are very bright, forthright, and outspoken. One, George, is referred to by colleagues as the Minister of Responsible Disturbance. It would be much easier to lead faculty meetings if these two faculty members were not there. At the same time, however, faculty meetings are more interesting and decisions are usually better because of their presence.

Some of the more bothersome contradictions facing educators are political and financial, including the following:

1. Our school's children are getting higher test scores, which pleases the parents and board of education, but are they really learning more or learning what is important to learn?
2. The board of education and superintendent constantly talk about the lack of financial resources, but hire consultants whose contribution is questionable.
3. When students in special situations achieve well, we lose federal funds.
4. Many teachers won't stay after school to hand out report cards, but they say they really care about children.

5. The best teachers are rewarded with jobs in central office.

6. They talk about teamwork in this school, but the most presti-
   gious honor is a solitary one—Teacher of the Year.

7. Boards of education choose leaders they think they can control.

8. Because of questionable teacher evaluation procedures, poor
   teachers survive.

9. Board members talk about hiring the best persons for jobs, but
   pressure us to nominate their own favorites for positions.

10. Board members and administrators talk about excellence, but
    those who "suck up" prosper.

Occasionally, a contradiction comes home in our personal lives, and
our rhetoric sounds hollow because of inconsistent actions. A teacher
of learning disabled (LD) students describes this experience: "I have
always been a strong advocate for my LD students, and my daughter has respected me for this. However, I was aghast when my daughter
wanted to date one of my LD students. I objected and my daughter said,
'Mom, you're a hypocrite.' "(This brings us to one of the most important
questions facing the educational leader: "Whose ox is being gored?")

Please take a moment to identify in the chart below those contradictions you expect to celebrate (or do celebrate) as a teacher and
those contradictions you expect will (or presently do) demand hard
psychological work. Then look at the following responses from
other educators to this assignment (page 43).

| *Column 1* | *Column 2* |
| *(celebrate)* | *(reconcile)* |

Column 1 (celebrate)	Column 2 (reconcile)
"We have excellent parent involvement and this means we give many of our resources (e.g., time and effort) to parents."	"I always feel like I'm the person in the middle."
"There are always more desires than resources, something I celebrate because we want people to be proactive."	"I appreciate the energy of young staff members, but many are really naive about what I, an experienced educator, can do."
"Because I have a proven track record, they call on me to do more than I sometimes want to do."	"Some teachers nag, which I don't like, and yet I admire commitment."
	"As a female educator I always confront (have to deal with) the 'old boys' club."

Although it is not always easy to do, it is good to remind ourselves that there is no movement without friction, and difficult contradictions provide such friction. They challenge us to learn more about ourselves from our interactions with others and the environment.

Conclusion

Doing one's professional autobiography and then sharing autobiographies with others can be one of the most rewarding experiences the creative curriculum leader can have. We get to know ourselves and others better—an important step in the creation of community. And, we can see what those special talents are that give us a sense of vocation or "calling."

Case 4: Personal Disclosure and the Leader's Credibility

You are at a seminar on curriculum leadership. There is a spirited discussion concerning whether leaders in an organization should deliberately create distance between self and others. One leader in your seminar presents a point of view with considerable forcefulness:

At the beginning of his administration, President Clinton took a select group of advisers to Camp David for a weekend retreat. The press reported that at this retreat a facilitator was working with the group, and President Clinton said that as a child he was called "chubby" and this negative labeling was very hurtful to him.

This is the kind of thing that demeans the office of the presidency. The head of an organization not only represents self but also the institution of the presidency. You have to keep distance between yourself and others, and this kind of behavior by the president works against the credibility of the president and the institution of the presidency.

Another leader at the seminar strongly disagrees with the first leader's statement: "I have even greater respect for President Clinton because of this. He has demonstrated that he is human and suffers at times just like the rest of us."

You are asked for your views on this matter. What will you say, and what is the rationale for your position? Please choose from the alternative rationales that follow:

1. The first speaker's position is correct. Distance must be kept between the leader and others in the organization.
2. The second speaker is correct and the first speaker is off base. Showing your feelings and being close to followers is simply being human.

*Case 4: Rationales for
the Alternative Responses*

1. President Clinton made a mistake in supporting a format with a facilitator. As President of the United States, he is the "boss" and he demeaned himself by stepping away from hierarchy. He should share such feelings in the privacy of his family but not outside of that institution. Some people will always take advantage of you if you let down your guard. Showing your emotions, particularly as a leader, scares a lot of people. President Clinton added to their fright by doing what he did. In summary, he made the mistake of stepping outside of his role.

2. This case is all about expectations—expectations one has of self, and others have of the leader. President Clinton's response was like a breath of fresh air. Most presidents have been out of touch with people and their own humanity. President Clinton has a right to hurt, just like everybody else. Sharing his feelings about being wronged is a sign of good mental health, and his presidency is better because of such disclosure. He also broke the stereotype that only women are nurturing leaders. He exhibited real courage and leadership in what he did.

Case 5: Caring and Caretaking

An experienced educator who is nearing retirement gives a speech at a leadership seminar in your school system. The following are some of the educator's comments that were made in a sincere and informal manner:

One thing I learned early as a leader is that there are a lot of breakdowns. Relationships between teachers, teachers and students, teachers and administrators, teachers and parents, and teachers and central office personnel sometimes break down.

For the first few years of my principalship, I fell into the trap of thinking that whenever something went wrong at school, it was my fault. For example, the superintendent visited our school when we had our annual carnival. A parent, who is also a friend of the superintendent, threw a soft whip pie in the superintendent's face. I didn't know how the superintendent would react and my immediate feeling was that I should have never let this happen. It's my fault that it happened. The fact that the superintendent was a good sport about this didn't eliminate my feeling.

After attending a workshop for principals on "knowing thyself," I began to see that there is a difference between caring and caretaking. As the oldest child in the family, I was responsible for taking care of my younger brothers and sisters, and I carried this attitude of control and responsibility into college, teaching, and the principalship.

I simply wanted to tell you this story of my breakthrough because I couldn't begin to understand others and myself until I was willing to give up much of this control.

You have listened to this story. What thoughts do you have about it? Please choose from the following alternative responses:

1. As the principal, the person in charge of the school, you give up efforts to control things at your own peril. Be courteous to the speaker but remind yourself that the message just isn't one that will work for you.

2. The principal is a wise person. Take the principal's words to heart and map out ways in which you can apply them to your leadership position.

3. Ignore the message as it is basically irrelevant.

Case 5: Rationales for the Alternative Responses

1. The basic message of many religions is that one should always do for others. Trying to control school situations to prevent any problems from occurring is simply what a good leader does. For example, the principal is right for feeling guilty about what happened to the superintendent. If something goes wrong, prepare yourself for trouble, because you are accountable. The difficulty with this response and rationale is the high price you will pay for having it. You will constantly have to give resources to being on guard, and worrying can get you down. Search for a better response.

2. The basic question this wise educator speaks to is "How shall I live with myself as well as others?" If you try to control everything you will be co-dependent because you will take the blame for everything that happens. One of the first things you try to teach parents of special children, for example, is that they must encourage special children to take risks so that they learn to do as much as possible for themselves. This is the best answer, and the educator near retirement has given you good advice in an authentic way.

3. Staying out of it or hiding can save resources for you as a leader. The problem with this rationale is that the issue of caring and caretaking is at the core of the leadership issue. Find a better response that demonstrates a more professional and committed attitude.

4

Looking Forward to Work
The Power of Wanting to Be There

*And if you sing though as angels, and love not the
singing, you muffle man's ears to the voices of the day
and the voices of the night.*

Kahlil Gibran (1923, p. 28)

A reading of students' professional autobiographies indicates that those who have "a sense of calling" and feel
good about using their talents look forward to going to work each
day. In being in touch with their histories, they feel that they can
make a difference in the lives of their students. Although it simply
makes sense that "there's no substitute for wanting to be there,"
one discovers little research and writing on this subject (Brubaker,
1986).

The subject came to my attention when our family went to a
restaurant. The hostess greeted us cordially and led us to our table,
which was in an inviting setting.

Our waitress approached our table and said, "Can I help you," in
a voice devoid of emotion. She wasn't unpleasant and she wasn't
pleasant. She was simply there. Our family reacted to her flattened
affect by trying to pick up her spirits with humor and caring comments. No response. The result of this lack of interaction with the
waitress, the leader who was expected to set the stage for a pleasant
evening, was that the food was excellent but the dining experience

was not. While riding home in the car, one of our children said, "The waitress acted as if she didn't want to be with us."

This experience stimulated my thinking about the importance of the leader sending a powerful message to followers: "I want to be with you." I suspect that each of us enters the work world daily asking questions like: "Does my boss think my contribution is special enough to want to be with me?" "Do my fellow workers value my work and want to be with me?" If the answer is "yes," the day seems a little shorter and the quality of work is better.

Teachers probably look to administrators, and children look to teachers, with the same question in mind: "Do you want to be with me?" When followers believe that the leader wants to be there with them, successful leadership is not necessarily assured; but, on the other hand, their belief that the leader doesn't want to be there certainly works against effective leadership.

With these thoughts in mind, I asked a Clemson University sophomore, who happened to be next to me on a flight from Greensboro to Boston, "How do you know during the first few minutes of a class if the professor wants to be with you?" At first, she had difficulty with the question since she had naturally not prepared herself to answer such a different query. But, once she got started, her answer was both clear and provocative:

The first thing I look at is the way the professor walks into the classroom. Is he [for example] standoffish, or does he look at the students? If he looks at the class, and particularly if he has eye contact with each student, the professor has something at stake.

Then I look to see if he expects us to work. There are several ways this is shown. Does he bring the textbook with him? If he does, this demonstrates the important place the book will have in the course.

If the professor brings in the book, does he place it on the table with respect or does he toss it down as if it's not very important?

I also listen to the firmness of his voice. If his voice is firm, this is a first step in telling us that he has high expectations.

The professor's energy level tells me he is interested in me. He must have a high energy level and still seem reasonably relaxed. He uses this energy to set high expectations, but his being reasonably relaxed tells me he thinks I can meet these expectations.

I can tell almost immediately if the professor expects interaction between himself and the students, and among students. Does he expect us to be passive, or does he encourage us to ask real questions that don't have easy answers? And, does he listen to our answers, or is he so glued to his notes that he isn't interested in learning from us?

I'm really bothered if the professor immediately plays favorites. If he does he is probably there for social reasons and not the course itself. He wants our approval.

At the end of the conversation, this bright, articulate university student passionately delivered a postscript:

You need to beware of something with us students. We need guidance, even to be told what to do at times, because we're scared of failure. The fewer decisions we make, the less risk of failure there is. Some of us are miserable and we see ourselves as victims because we see others having so much compared to us. You have a challenge with us: If you can, move us beyond these feelings to accept responsibility.

The conviction in the student's answer to my initial question said a great deal. She shared the simple but powerful truth that our enthusiasm for our work keeps us from becoming cynical—the deadliest of leadership qualities. A 19-year-old reminded me that as creative curriculum leaders, we have at our fingertips an obvious and often overlooked source of power—wanting to be there.

My conversation with this university student stimulated me to think more about leadership qualities that work for and against wanting to be there—at work. The centerpiece for wanting to be there appears to be one's passion for learning. There seems to be a yearning on the part of educators to somehow recapture the curiosity, awe, wonder, and amazement we had when we started school. Adults have vivid memories of early discoveries. A principal in New Mexico said, "When I was a first grader I saw leaves on trees. They were so green and I wondered where they came from and why they danced in the wind." Another educator added, "When I saw my first caterpillar I let it crawl up and down my arm. I was six."

Curiosity and a sense of exploration drive us forward and lead to new understandings. An experienced teacher from Arizona described her engagement in the creative process:

> When I was 10 years old we got our first television set from the Firestone Store and we watched "I Love Lucy." I had my nose up to the screen, which taught my parents that I had eye trouble. I got glasses a week later. This made it possible for me to walk away from my mother in the grocery store for the first time—I could see.

Curiosity totally immerses a person in the joy of learning. Time and place take a backseat to the excitement of the moment. Listen to some more comments from adult educators who were asked to recall a childhood experience where they were driven by a sense of exploration and a passion for learning:

> When I was 7 or 8 my Dad let me use his bamboo fishing pole. I could fish for myself. I caught and ate 17 bluegills. The bobber kept going under. My brothers couldn't believe their sister caught all of these fish. Everybody said, "How wonderful!"

> I rode a train as a second grader. I had life space away from my family.

> The first time I snorkeled I was 5 years old. The bluefish kept touching me.

> I remember the first day of school—the sounds, smells, colors. The room was clean and neat.

> I'll never forget the first day I learned to drive in the driveway. I was 13.

> I remember listening to my cousin being born. I was 6 and stood outside and beneath the window. I saw my aunt with the baby on her lap. My aunt had a flat stomach again.

I rode an escalator in Birmingham when I was 12. We only had a one-story house in Enterprise, Alabama, and so this was a totally different experience for me.

I felt the warmth and saw the glow of the volcano 30 miles away. Where did everything go? I wondered. . . .

When students were asked what characterized their being turned on to learning where they experienced awe, wonder and amazement, they responded as follows:

A sense of humor;

Risk taking, breaking routine, tradition, and ritual;

Hope;

A caring attitude toward self, others, and the challenge;

Inner strength that comes from courage, commitment, and conviction;

The feeling of being "infected"—totally absorbed;

A sensitive attitude that allowed me to *sense* everything around me;

The desire to do whatever I was doing well;

The fact that I was prepared to learn—a matter of mindset;

Perseverance; and

The pure delight that comes from meeting the challenge.

As creative curriculum leaders who are developing our own curricula, we face a question of great importance: "How can I make a difference in the lives of others and myself, so that we create environments that stimulate the qualities of exploration and learning listed above?" Wanting to be there is a significant first step in realizing our vocation or "calling." Continuing to want to be there or "keeping the fire" is the subject of the next chapter.

Case 6: Parent Contradicts Self
in Speech to Faculty

You have been appointed as chair of the staff development committee. The parent of one of the students in your school is a prominent businessman in your community and a dynamic speaker. You have invited him to speak to the faculty at the beginning of the year on the subject "A Parent's View of School Reform."

The speaker begins with a brief sketch of his life, from its origins on a farm to his present position of prominence in his region of the country. He outlines the secret to success in general and his success in particular: (a) the ability to hustle—set goals and go after them; (b) perseverance; (c) people skills; and (d) excellent follow-through. He speaks with passion about how he graduated from the "school of hard knocks," with his ability to draw from his many and diverse experiences as the main key to his success.

Then he moves to a critique of the schools. He argues that schools have neglected the basics of reading, writing, and mathematics. He elaborates by saying that schools should get rid of the frills and give attention only to the basic subjects.

Later in the day your superintendent asks for your views on the speaker's presentation. The superintendent wasn't able to attend the speech. What will you say? Please choose the best of the following alternative responses:

1. The overall message communicated by the speaker verbally and nonverbally is that he has been successful because he has "wanted to be there." People skills, hard work, setting goals, and follow-through are the keys to his passion for his work. This message is so strong and important that the contradiction in relation to his expectations for curriculum is of little consequence. Relate the first part of his message to the superintendent as an example of the power of "wanting to be there" and leave it at that.

2. The first part of the speaker's message is correct, but he contradicts himself by advocating a view of curriculum that simply doesn't fit. Point this out to the superintendent but do so without being hypercritical.

3. Tell the superintendent that the speaker did a good job without referring to any specific content of the speech.

Case 6: Rationales for
the Alternative Responses

1. The main part of the speaker's message is one that your superintendent can communicate to others—even the speaker himself, if the superintendent talks to him. The difficulty with this response and rationale is that the superintendent won't have a sense of the total message of the speech if critics speak to the superintendent about the speech. Find a better response.

2. Your balanced description and critique of the speech will give the superintendent total context. The speaker's solution of returning to the basics contradicts his earlier remarks. Basic instruction emphasizes product (i.e., content) rather than process (such as goal setting). You might add that self-made business people sometimes fail to see this contradiction. Your providing total context communicates trust in the superintendent's ability to use the information you provide wisely. This is probably the best response.

3. A general surface view of the speech will keep you out of any controversy that the speech may have caused. Hiding can sometimes be wise. The problem with this response and rationale is that the superintendent can be blindsided by critics' comments with regard to the speech. You will come across to the superintendent, in this event, as a person with little expertise and conviction. In short, you won't appear to be a professional.

5

Keeping the Fire in Your Vocation

Arthur Ashe has always been a student of himself and his
surroundings, a man engaged by the world, sure of himself.

Frank Deford (1992, p. 62)

A sense of vocation or calling must be nurtured on a consistent basis. Such nurturing doesn't simply happen, but must be cultivated or sought out by the creative curriculum leader. As might be suspected, "Boredom is the deadliest poison and it is a truism that it strikes hardest at the most comfortable" (Buckley, 1976, p. 26). And hard on the heels of boredom often comes cynicism, a deadly and cowardly form of superiority.

Proactive creative leadership is one antidote to boredom and cynicism, for it challenges us to use our talents to encourage others to do likewise. Creative leadership places us at the center of the action, for it helps us resolve the mental tug-of-war that each of us feels between two opposing forces: "Get involved!" versus "Hold back!" Those who opt for getting involved recognize that creative leadership can be a celebration of our ability to make a difference.

What are the steps one takes to meet this creative leadership challenge and "keep the fire?" First, in Chapter 3, "Learning From Your Professional Autobiography," we saw that it is helpful to ask the question, "What are my special talents?" Using one's talents is a matter of interest and proficiency. The possible distinction between interest and proficiency was brought to my attention by

Gerald Austin, a National Football League referee and education consultant. As I left his office, I said to him, "How about you making the phone call to the superintendent of schools? I'm not good at that sort of thing." Gerald responded, "No, you're good at it but you just don't especially enjoy doing it." He was right. I had little interest in or desire to make the call.

There can be a good deal of pressure associated with being expected to do well at something you're good at. For example, one of the reasons I enjoy the exercise of swimming so much is that I'm not expected to be good at it. It is simply a matter of swimming laps at my own speed, using an adequate but not outstanding swimming stroke. In playing tennis, however, there is often a certain kind of pressure associated with being good at it. I consider it and others consider it to be my sport.

It is important for the creative curriculum leader to remember the possible distinction between proficiency and interest in developing your own curriculum, as well as curriculum as a course of study. Those we are expected to lead may want to try out different challenges, even though they don't feel especially comfortable or talented in these areas. Others may not want to use a particular talent, even though all within the setting know they are good at using this talent. This came to my attention in a school that was moving toward shared decision making. A teacher had recently moved into the system from Florida, where she had been a very successful teacher and school leader. I therefore assumed that she would welcome my invitation to serve as one of the grade level leaders in the school. She looked at me with a somewhat pained expression and said, "I would rather not as my plate is full with other responsibilities and I want to try out different challenges than those I met in my last school." "Fair enough," I responded and added, "I appreciate your honest response and I respect the fact that you don't see yourself as a superwoman who has to say yes to every invitation."

The second step in meeting the leadership challenge and keeping the fire is demonstrated by the teacher who refused my invitation. She decided what she wanted to focus on in order to actively seek opportunities to improve the use of these talents. The mistake some people make is to ride off in all directions. This can lead to the feeling that nothing is being done well. How do you prevent this? By identifying organizations and settings within organizations that are especially important to you.

The third step is a transitional one, moving from passive spectator to active spectator. A university student described this transitional step: "I decided to sit in the T in the front of the class and occasionally stop in to discuss matters of mutual interest with the professor." She added, "At first I thought of this as just 'sucking up' but the interesting thing I discovered is that professors are pretty lonely people who usually enjoy talking to students." "And," she went on to say, "I took a new interest in the class because I had taken the initiative." Her activities had new focus and meaning—and she got a higher grade than she normally earned.

The fourth step achieved by the university student was to identify leadership skills that stretched her to find new uses for her talents. Although she was nervous when she initiated contact with her professor, she learned that she had networking skills she didn't know she had. She was able to articulate her ideas and feelings in an informal setting. Those who underestimate their talents experience the fear of feeling not quite good enough. Those who overestimate their talents don't know what they don't know, and therefore can't set about to learn it.

Now that you have identified those leadership skills you want to improve, the final step is to practice, practice, practice. The place to begin is with mundane assignments others often refuse: taking minutes at meetings, serving as chair of the social committee, running the projector, and introducing speakers. These opportunities give you practice and place you near the center of the action and power. A person who attended one of our leadership seminars described his experience in taking minutes:

> The chair of the committee asked who wanted to take the minutes, heads turned downward and no one volunteered. I said that I would. I discovered that I could write interesting and sometimes humorous notes, and this record was always read at the beginning of each meeting, thus setting the tone for the committee's work. I was part of the action.

The amazing thing about practice is that it leads to self-confidence and enjoyment. And there is a bonus, best expressed by Gary Player: "The harder I practice, the luckier I get" (Brubaker, 1988, p. 8).

The personal and professional rewards in meeting this creative curriculum leadership challenge are many, but perhaps the most satisfying one is to participate in something larger than oneself, for it is in using those talents that interest us that we create each other in community.

Guidelines for Keeping the Fire

The five steps discussed thus far in this chapter are complemented by the following guidelines for keeping the fire. Enjoy your secret aspirations, for they are images that will drive you forward and map your future. A prominent newscaster described the role of secret aspirations he held as a child: "My parents divorced when I was in my early teens and so I was sent to a small town in West Virginia with my father, who was an alcoholic. There was many a night when I would pull my father out of a snowbank near our front door." He added, "I sat at my school desk and thought about how I would get out of this situation and make a better life for myself. A few caring teachers shared my dream and made a difference in my life." The newscaster's dream was at first a general direction, something he creatively brooded about before seeing specific details that would lead to concrete action (Brubaker & Kinard, 1988).

A second guideline is to start wherever you are right now to set new directions. It is a delusion to think that you can jump right to the top and be an accomplished performer. The prominent newscaster's career began with a radio audition in a small town, at which he was asked to read three items: a commercial, a public service announcement and an obituary. He didn't get the announcer's position, but instead was offered a job sweeping floors and filing records at $7.50 a week. This gave him access to the station's control board and the opportunity to practice radio announcing.

A creative curriculum leader was bothered by anxiety over speech making to the extent that he was losing sleep. He talked to a friend who is a nationally recognized public speaker. The friend said, "The place to start learning to speak better is in any group that will invite you." The anxious speaker took his advice and began speaking at local civic groups and the like. After several years of practice, he is not an outstanding speaker but he is good enough so that he sleeps better.

The third guideline is that there is no substitute for spontaneity. Pretension is the enemy of authenticity, a key to creative leadership. M. Scott Peck (1993) speaks to the matter of pretension and rigidity: "Most of the evil in this world—the incivility—is committed by people who are absolutely certain that they know what they're doing" (p. 91).

It sounds ironic, but the secret to spontaneity (and enjoying yourself) is not to take any one thing too seriously. To do so is to lose one's sense of humor. An educator said to me, "The best time I ever had was when I was roasted at a banquet when I announced my retirement." He had learned to laugh at life and himself.

Concentrating on the task at hand can be another way of keeping the fire. This takes attention off of yourself and allows the natural warmth of your personality to come forward. Whether you are talking to a group or an individual, make eye contact and speak from your heart. Warmth and confidence will follow.

One also keeps the fire alive by passing the torch to others. We feel the pride of ownership when we give our creative energies to what we value, but this pride is empty if we don't have others to share what we are creating. Each of us can remember someone who saw in us talents that we didn't recognize in ourselves. And we are challenged to pass on this gift to others. The previously mentioned newscaster felt this in his first speech class: "I had an exceptional teacher who reassured me from those first embarrassing moments in giving a speech in class that I could do it."

Another guideline rarely discussed is that there is no substitute for having someone who loves you unconditionally. It is not fashionable, particularly for men, to talk about love as the driving force in their lives. And yet, conversations with men in leadership seminars have taught us that the support of significant caring people in their lives has made all of the difference. Giving our resources to creating bridges rather than walls moves us away from a zero-sum way of seeing others. The more we give to each other, the more we seem to get from each other.

How Will I Know if the Fire Is Alive?

First, the anxiety of actually doing things will subside as the process of doing them unfolds. Second, your resources will be devoted to building, rather than tearing down. You will feel less inclined to criticize others and will enjoy what you're doing more. Third, others' opinions of how you perform will be less important than your own enjoyment of it. Trying to please everybody is an impossible and frustrating goal.

The metaphor of banking the coals in old-fashioned iron stoves to preserve the fire on the most frigid nights is a useful one. When you go to bed at night, concentrate on banking the coals in your mind. Allow the brain, a marvelous instrument, to create new concepts while you sleep. And, think of the seemingly mundane acts you perform each day as a creative curriculum leader as banking the coals for more critical tasks ahead. There are also times when problems seem to overwhelm us. Distance and reflection have a way of creating avenues to their own resolution. Morning often brings a refreshing interpretation to the quandary of the previous day. Banking the fire for problem resolution is far more profitable than dwelling on a problem, as many of us are prone to do. Time, distance, reflection, and interpretation allow the embers of the fire the space to create new and more distinct images of life's challenges.

Conclusion

You will be motivated to further your vocation or calling, and develop your curriculum, by knowing ways to keep the fire. Because of the uniqueness of each person, there is no one set of steps or guidelines that will work for all educators. Rather, it is our challenge to find those ways that work for us as individuals. And it is the sharing of what we learn through this process that once again helps us create community.

Case 7: Contradictory Messages
About Motivation for Teaching

You have attended one of the best orientation speeches by a superintendent of schools. Several thousand teachers and administrators applauded the superintendent for his stirring message. The central part of his speech was that the buzz words of education, such as "Site-Based Management" and "Outcome-Based Education," are not the heart of education. The real motivation for teaching, according to the superintendent, is your relationship as a teacher with children in the classroom and school.

You return to your school for the orientation meeting conducted by the principal. The principal, who is very poised and articulate, gives a motivational speech on the new Site-Based Management plan for organizing the school, and the new Outcome-Based Education program she has been exposed to over the summer. Emphasis is on these programs as the solution to problems in the school rather than on the relationship between the teacher and students.

After lunch you return to the school to discuss the morning's activities with your leadership team. What will you say? Please choose from the following alternatives:

1. The superintendent is right. Take the message to heart and ignore the principal's speech.
2. The principal's message is the one you live with each day. Take her message to heart and ignore the superintendent's speech.
3. You know by now that contradictory messages are par for the course. Do what you think is right as a professional person.

Case 7: Rationales for
the Alternative Responses

1. The superintendent is obviously right. There are so many buzz words surrounding education that you know by now that programs attached to them come and go. To depend on such buzz words and programs to keep the fire leads to a superficial professional style. However, to simply try to implement the superintendent's speech without further reflection fails to consider the culture of your school. Consider a better response.

2. It is certainly true that you have to live with your principal as the primary person who sets the tone for the culture of your school. However, you also know from experience that your principal will begin each year by trying to implement the most recent buzz words

and programs. To simply try to implement the principal's most recent message is to live a superficial life, adjusting to this externally located authority. Seek a better response.

3. Motivation, or keeping the fire, has to be internally located to really make a difference. The superintendent's message is on target, and the principal is off base. Take this information and point of view to your leadership committee and use it as the basis for discussion. You will have to participate in the principal's most recent pet programs, but recognize that you as a professional person are the artist who will make a difference in relating to students and colleagues. This is the best response.

Case 8: Colleague Asks Advice About Dealing With Anxiety and Depression

A colleague and friend at work takes you aside after the school day is over and says the following to you:

> I am one of the few school principals who left the principalship to return to teaching. I never told you all of the reasons why I left the principalship and I haven't told you what has happened to me since I left the principalship. When the principalship got to me I said, "Why am I responsible for all of these irresponsible people?" What I really meant was that there seemed to be no getting away from the responsibility of the job. I never learned to pace myself. I remember the day that I sat down and typed out my resignation. A great sense of relief came over me.
>
> What I didn't expect is what I am experiencing now. Even though I got a letter from the superintendent of schools, saying what a good job I did, and even though I always got high evaluations at the end of each year, *I feel like I failed.* I still can't sleep well at night and I am starting to develop phobias that seem to overcome me at times. When I was a principal I suffered from anxiety, but now I really feel depressed. What should I do?

Please choose the best of the following alternatives:

1. Listen to your friend carefully and support your friend in any way short of giving specific advice.

2. Listen to your friend carefully, give support, and recommend talking to the principal.

3. Listen to your friend carefully, give support, and recommend talking to his or her family physician.

4. Listen to your friend carefully, give support, recommend talking to his or her family physician, but add that he or she may wish to also talk to a psychologist, counselor, or psychiatrist if the family physician isn't very helpful.

Case 8: Rationales for the Alternative Responses

1. By listening to your friend carefully you will be giving support but you won't hazard possible difficulties of giving advice. In a matter like this, only experts can give advice, and you aren't an expert. The problem with this response is that your friend is asking for advice and appears to be suffering a good deal. By not meeting his request you may communicate a lack of support. Consider other alternatives for a better response.

2. By listening to your friend and giving advice you will demonstrate your concern and care. Your recommendation to talk to his or her principal may or may not be a good idea, depending on the principal. If the principal is a competent and caring person, it will be helpful to have the designated leader's support at work. If the principal is insensitive, or worse yet the kind of leader who could hold this over your friend's head, it would be a serious mistake to talk to the principal at this point, or perhaps at any point. The possible difficulties with this response should probably prompt you to advise looking at other alternatives.

3. Listening and caring are important first steps. Your friend's description of his or her pain and request for advice should tell you that more serious measures are called for. The family physician should know something about situations like this and is also bound by professional code to discretion. The family physician also has a medical network in place and can recommend a psychiatrist or psychologist if necessary. The drawback with this option is that the family physician may or may not be expert enough in such matters

to help your friend. Some are and some aren't. Therefore, consider a better response.

4. Listening to your friend and caring is a very important first step. Your friend's honest sharing of information regarding anxiety and depression plus his or her request for advice indicates your friend is serious about the pain and difficulties. Therefore, advise your friend to seek professional help in the event that the family physician doesn't give advice that eases the pain and helps your friend feel better. Make it clear that you will support him or her by caring and being a good listener at any time during counseling. This is probably the best response, although alternative 3 is also a good response.

PART III Curriculum Development Can Make a Difference

It is simply a truism that educators exist within organizations, and one's attitudes are part of larger mindsets (paradigms) toward such organizations. Occasionally, there is a radical change in an educator's mindset, something that may be called a *paradigm shift*. Gerald Austin, former superintendent of schools and a National Football League referee, describes a paradigm shift that occurred after reading *Creative Survival in Educational Bureaucracies* (Brubaker & Nelson, 1974). As he explained it, "I used to think I was severely constricted by organizations. Then I realized that *once you know what the rules are, everything else is open to you*" (Austin, 1993).

Austin implies that there are three dimensions to leadership: (1) *what is*, including what the rules are; (2) *what should be*, one's personal and organizational vision; and (3) *what can be*, the art of the possible or the political. These three aspects of decision making lead us to the power of knowing how to critique. That is, the decision maker reviews what is going on, adopts a point of view in relation to what is observed, and then supports this point of view in light of what is possible. A superintendent of schools describes this process:

I had only been on the job for 3 months when asked to appear on a half-hour television news program. While on the way to the station, the deputy superintendent asked me what I planned to say. I replied, "It all boils down to this. This system has had a history of hiring people because they are someone's relatives or friends. This practice has not been in the best interest of children and the system as a whole. Under my administration we're going to hire the best qualified person for the job. Excellent schools depend on hiring excellent staff and I'm going to use all of the resources I have to build an excellent school system."

The superintendent of schools didn't always get his way on this matter with the school board, but his realistic critique of the situation he inherited was a kind of map for daily decision making. His personal and organizational vision served as a beacon of light that guided him through troubled waters. In short, he had integrity, a basic element of character (Covey, 1989). He had defined and empowered himself (Steinem, 1992). His personal curriculum development was the substructure for creative leadership in the school system. He demonstrated that critique, as with all evaluation, *is personal*.

Chapter 6, "Creative Curriculum Leadership in Practice," discusses what happens when the educator interested in developing his or her own curriculum applies such knowledge to learning settings. This chapter weds the inner curriculum and the outer curriculum: what each person experiences as learning settings are cooperatively created, and the course of study. Chapter 7, "Civility in Leadership: The Ultimate Difference," describes what happens in learning settings when educators give attention to the character issue. It is argued that such attention makes all the difference in the kinds of relationships professional educators and others experience.

6

Creative Curriculum Leadership in Practice

In college I used my intellectual skills to get good grades by knowing the right answers. But at work, I found out that knowing the right answer was only 10 percent of the battle. Working with people was the other 90 percent. And we hadn't learned that at school.

Quoted in McCall, Lombardo, and Morrison (1988, p. 22)

The above quote is from a college graduate who described the shift from the culture of higher education to the culture of the work world. For our purposes, the graduate makes the point that human endeavor, rather than scientific pursuit, is at the center of creative curriculum leadership. It has been argued in this book that the creative curriculum leader uses his or her talents to help others identify and use their talents. And this role for the curriculum leader is quite different from the role commonly prescribed; namely, the leader gets others to do what he or she wants them to do, regardless of whether they want to do it. The commonly prescribed role has a "scientific management" ring to it— the ring of manipulation and top-down power arrangements.

We will see in this chapter that the creative curriculum leader is challenged to establish lateral relationships with others, so that they are empowered to own new directions for themselves within the organizational structure of schools and school systems.

We begin our discussion of creative curriculum leadership by describing and discussing four kinds of covenants or relationships with persons that vary with respect to *intensity* and *duration* (Brubaker, 1982). We enter into covenants with other persons in order to assure predictability in our relationships. Entering into an agreement to play tennis with another person is a useful metaphor. Players agree to accept certain "rules of the game" so that one's expertise, rather than one's ability to cheat, is at stake: The boundaries of the court are lined, a ball that falls on a line is playable, the player serving has two serves per point, and so forth. In short, one's flexibility or choice of options is diminished in the interest of predictability, but this predictability in turn assures players of a kind of freedom since less time and emotional effort are needed than would be the case if chaos prevailed.

A similar situation exists for the curriculum leader. Dependable relationships help the curriculum leader distinguish between the possible and the impossible. The head of a curriculum committee needs to know which members of the committee will probably attend meetings, and also needs to assess their abilities and commitments, in order to know what they can be expected to do if certain tasks are to be completed. Committee members need similar information about the curriculum leader.

Covenant 1: Little Intensity and Brief Duration

Our technologically advanced society encourages many covenants that are pleasant but taken lightly. They also don't last very long. The seasoned airplane passenger experiences this kind of covenant. Flight attendants and others are pleasant and, in fact, frequently act as if they are creating another home setting for the customer. If you recognized a flight attendant in a department store later in the day, you probably wouldn't go out of your way to say hello in spite of congenial rhetoric earlier in the day.

As a curriculum leader you may be asked to give a brief speech that introduces the audience to the curriculum-planning process. Or you may be asked to either head or be a member of an ad hoc curriculum group that meets briefly, simply to justify an already made decision by an administrator. Both of these situations are examples of covenants of little intensity and brief duration.

Covenant 2: High Intensity and Brief Duration

If you are an infrequent airplane passenger who is anxious about flying, the 30-minute flight is probably very intense, in spite of its brief duration. I encountered such a person on a flight from Williamsport, Pennsylvania, to Philadelphia. He drank his own two alcoholic beverages as well as two ordered by his wife before slowly disembarking from the airplane.

As a curriculum leader you may be asked to be a member of an accreditation team that makes an on-site visit to a host organization for a few days. Team members immerse themselves in the evaluation process literally night and day. The importance of the task draws team members into a close working relationship, at the end of which a report is written and members go their separate ways. Another example is a curriculum retreat, where persons work closely together in a relatively isolated setting for a brief period of time. There is often an adjustment period when participants return to their home settings and find that such settings have a life of their own that is quite different from the retreat setting.

Covenant 3: Not Intense but Long-Term

A curriculum leader may be assigned to a committee that has a ritualistic function, which must be carried out infrequently for the year or for several years. The commencement committee in a very tradition-oriented setting serves as an example. Some committees that give scholarships to students are also of this nature. They meet several times during the year to make decisions about who gets what scholarships, but their deliberations are largely perfunctory, as are the deliberations of the commencement committee that meets several times a year and simply affirms traditionally made decisions.

Covenant 4: Intense and Long-Term

The final kind of covenant is the rarest. You, the curriculum leader, may be assigned to a long-range planning committee that is expected to meet for 3 years. During this time you meet almost weekly and make a number of difficult decisions that will affect persons in the organization. For example, you may recommend the elimination of some programs and the diminution of others—decisions that affect the lives of organization members as well as their families and friends.

You are probably at the place where you wonder how the covenant framework is useful to you as a creative curriculum leader. In order to help others identify and use their talents, the creative curriculum leader is aware of the opportunities each kind of covenant offers. For example, Covenant 1, little intensity and brief duration, gives people with ritualistic talents a chance to use them. Some people are truly gifted in ceremonial roles. They are able to stand up, often on a moment's notice, and represent your school or school system well. Covenant 2, high intensity and brief duration, affords some people a chance to operate under pressure for a brief time, after which they can move on to the next challenge. Unlike the tortoise, the hare runs in spurts. So, too, do some curriculum leaders show their excellence in brief, pressure-packed situations. People with these talents usually do best in ad hoc task-oriented situations, where reports are due. Covenant 3, low intensity but long-term, also gives people with ritualistic talents the opportunity to stand up, speak eloquently, and then move back. Faculty meetings are sometimes led by people with these talents. Some educators handle details well when there is little pressure. They do well with Covenant 3 activities. Covenant 4, intense and long-term, demands curriculum leaders who will stay the course and have good follow-through. The intense nature of the long-term commitment demands leaders who are not fickle or rigid and who handle pressure well. Primarily, this kind of covenant calls for a person with well-honed people skills (Brubaker & Simon, 1993).

It should be clear that the curriculum leader's attitude toward a particular person or committee dictates the kind of covenant that is formed. For example, if a school principal strongly believes in Site-Based Management (SBM), the SBM leadership team or committee will probably enter into a highly intense and long-term covenant with the principal and one another. If the principal views SBM as a ritualistic requirement by the superintendent, the SBM committee will enter into a low-intensity but long-term covenant with the principal and one another.

It is also the case that a formally designated committee, such as the SBM leadership team, will sometimes simply fail to deliver over the course of a fairly long period of time, after which the principal will turn to another committee to do the job. For example, in one school where I was a consultant, the SBM committee turned into a "gripe group" because half of its members refused to think positively. They were experiencing difficult home situations that spilled over into their school lives. The principal worked with the team diligently, trying to help overcome the negativism, but her intervention didn't work. The principal, therefore, turned to the social committee as her core group or governance group, and the school climate improved considerably. This simply demonstrates that there is no one generalization that holds for all people in all situations. The principal and other curriculum leaders must have contingency plans and use their artistry.

The covenant framework may also be useful to the curriculum leader as an evaluation device. The creative curriculum leader can diagnose present relationships in a setting, some of which involve him or her, and others which involve other persons. The framework is also helpful in evaluating relationships that emerge during involvement in the curriculum development process. The curriculum leader can see how many and what kinds of relationships have formed in his or her own and others' professional lives. The framework can also serve the creative curriculum leader in planning for relationships he or she would like to see exist.

The previous discussion demonstrates that the creative curriculum leader knows that reaching important goals is not a solitary activity. It is therefore necessary to create a core group, whose members' commitment to each other is both intense and long-lasting (Covenant 4). Core group members are in effect a leadership team who afford emotional support and serve as a sounding board for sharpening ideas. In short, core group members are engaged in praxis, or reflective action, in the community.

In conclusion, the creative curriculum leader is aware of the value of all four kinds of covenants and initiates or participates in each to the best of his or her ability. It is a basic tenet of contingency theory that one's best choice of alternatives depends on the specific variables in a given situation (Peck, 1993).

Six Ways of Relating to Others

Stephen Covey, author of the excellent book, *The 7 Habits of Highly Effective People*, identifies six paradigms or mindsets of human interaction (1989). The creative curriculum leader can use this framework to identify and assess his or her leadership patterns as well as the patterns of others. Before identifying and describing the six ways of interacting with others, I would like to introduce a simulation game that will place you in the role of decision maker within the six-part framework. This game, "swimming the Amazon," is one I use in leadership seminars. It is based on an annual event in my swimming group.

Imagine for a moment that you are a respectable but not outstanding swimmer, who swims a mile five times a week in an after-school adult swimming group. There are approximately 10 other swimmers in your group. When you arrive at the pool on a Monday evening in January, the head lifeguard hands out a photocopied sheet with the headline "Welcome to the Amazon River Swim." The sheet explains that if you are interested in joining this swim, you should sign a sheet on the bulletin board at the end of the pool. Then, it is noted, you will be assigned a colored stick pin with your initials written on masking tape at the top of the pin. Your challenge is to swim the Amazon River, 25 miles in the pool, over a 6-week period. It is each participant's job as an "honor swimmer" to move his or her pin to the next mile mark on the bulletin board's drawing of the Amazon River. The sheet concludes by saying that you will receive a free T-shirt when your pin reaches the end (mouth) of the Amazon River.

You decide to accept the challenge and sign your name on the entrance sheet. The next day your pin is at the bottom of the Amazon River, and at the end of each swim you move your pin forward, toward the end of the river at the top of the bulletin board. You don't pay much attention to other pins on the board until, lo and behold, you see that your pin has reached the top of the bulletin board before all other pins reach this place.

What will you do with your pin? Why? If you are reading this in a solitary setting, please write your answers to the questions above. If you are in a group setting, share with the group your answers to these questions.

Let us now identify and describe six ways of interacting with others, after which you will be asked to locate your response, to where you will place your pin, in one of the categories.

Win/Win leaves all parties in the interaction with a good feeling about the decision and a common commitment to this decision and concrete next steps. The general mindset is one of cooperation rather than competition. Covey (1989) argues that "most situations, in fact, are part of an interdependent reality, and then Win/Win is really the only viable alternative" (p. 211).

Win/Lose places you in a position where you always compare your results to those of others. "No recognition is given to intrinsic value; everyone is extrinsically defined" (Covey, p. 208). Life is viewed as an arena where competition is both inevitable and desirable. Athletic contests are the most prominent metaphor for the Win/Lose paradigm, for there is clearly a winner and a loser. Covey concludes: "Certainly there is a place for Win/Lose thinking in truly competitive and low-trust situations. But most of life is not a competition" (pp. 208-209).

Lose/Win people are frequently happy only when they are pleasing and receiving the approbation of others. In order to compensate for their own lack of confidence, they live through the victories of others. "But the problem," according to Covey, "is that Lose/Win people bury a lot of feelings." He adds, "And unexpressed feelings never die: they're buried alive and come forth later in uglier ways" (p. 209).

Lose/Lose people are usually rigid, stubborn, and ego-invested (Covey, 1989). "Misery loves company" people are also often Lose/Lose people, for they only find direction in joining losing causes with like-minded people.

Win people "don't necessarily want someone else to lose. That's irrelevant; what matters is that they get what they want" (Covey, p. 210). As one leader said, "My philosophy is to get out front and then let others see what I've accomplished."

Win/Win or *No Deal* people agree to disagree agreeably (Covey, 1989). They simply don't want to make a deal. In short, they refuse to play the competitive game. They sometimes communicate the feeling that "I'm above the game by refusing to play it," or they simply go away so as to not get in the fray.

Please turn to the chart that follows and place your answers to the Amazon River Swim Game in the box that best defines your response. If you are in a group setting, place the names of others in your group in respective boxes after discussing in the group where such responses fall.

After you have participated in the first part of this exercise, imagine that you have just been named the principal of a school of your choice, or superintendent of a school system of your choice. Most new leaders are allowed to hire one trusted person from their old setting as a high-level assistant in the new setting. *Who in your group setting will you hire and why?* (Their responses to the Amazon River Swim Game must be used as the basis for your decision.)

You may be interested in some other participants' responses to the Amazon River Swim Game:

Win/Win people often say, "I would leave my pin at the mouth of the Amazon and wait for others. I may even slow myself down so that we can cross the line together. I believe in team victories."

Win/Lose participants say things like: "I would start over again with my pin and see how many others I could lap. Or else I would place my pin at the top left side of the bulletin board, with the number 1 to the left of my name, which I would spell out in large letters."

Lose/Win people often make comments like: "My satisfaction would come in seeing others cross the finish line. I would especially like to see some of the slower swimmers do well. Let someone else get eaten by the alligators. Others would be inspired and shocked to see me win."

Win swimmers say that their finishing first would be recognized and appreciated by themselves as winners. "I would just leave my pin at the top of the board," a Win participant said. She added, "I would get no satisfaction in seeing that others didn't finish first. That would be mean."

Win/Win or *No Deal* people simply refuse to say what they will do with their pins if all who play can't be winners. The game isn't worth playing if there have to be winners and losers.

There tend to be two general patterns in choosing an assistant in the new setting. The newly chosen principal or superintendent either chooses someone who has the same orientation to interacting

WIN/WIN	WIN/LOSE	LOSE/WIN
LOSE/LOSE	WIN	WIN/WIN OR NO DEAL

Amazon River Swim Game

with others, or someone who has a very different style that will complement the organizational head's style.

Now that you have participated in the Amazon River Swim Game and have placed responses in the six-part interaction framework, what guidelines can you identify for relating competition and cooperation to each other?

The following guidelines have been generated by leadership seminar participants:

1. Know who you are in relation to competition and cooperation.
2. Be all that you can be. You have to be able to compete and be a team player. Don't feel guilty if you win. (You don't need to pay interest on a debt you don't owe.)
3. Be yourself. Don't pretend to be someone you aren't. Enjoy who you are and be able to laugh at some of the funny things that happen because of who you are.
4. Be patient. The race went to the tortoise, not the hare.

A Sense of Vision

The creative curriculum leader is expected to give attention to both personal and organizational vision. As Lloyd DuVall (1989) said, "If you don't care where you are going, any trip will do!" But, adults and children interested in a school are not content to have leaders who are simply happy wanderers. Members within the school culture want to assign meaning to their activities, and it is this sense of direction or vision that can, if developed and articulated well, provide such meaning. Father Theodore Martin Hesburgh, president of the University of Notre Dame from 1952 to 1987, said it best: "The very essence of leadership is you have to have a vision. You can't blow an uncertain trumpet" (Austin & Brubaker, 1988, p. 104). When there is a shared vision, all are proud to be part of the organization. This serves as an essential element in self-management. The creative leader helps to create the conditions whereby others become their own leaders. They are motivated to give their best because they are on a team that is committed to important values. The value of such teamwork was related to the author by a teacher who headed the school's advisory council: "If there is no teamwork, everybody wastes resources in covering their backsides; when there is teamwork, trust replaces suspicion, people are willing to make themselves vulnerable and clear lines of communication exist."

Vision can sometimes help people in dramatic difficulty. Stephen Callahan spent 76 lonely days at sea after his sailboat capsized. How did he make it through his despair? "Dreams, ideas, and plans not only are an escape, they give me purpose, a reason to hang on" (Callahan, 1986, p. 63). Creative curriculum leaders also find a sense of vision helpful to them when times are tough—for example, when there are interpersonal difficulties with a principal or superintendent of schools. But, vision is equally important to us as we do the simple, mundane things each day. Actor Richard Dreyfuss talks about the importance of his vision of growing up and maturing: "It's thrilling. I enjoy even doing little things that I disdained before, like color-coordinating what I'm wearing, not looking like a jerk. It's the simple pleasure of behaving like a normal human being" (Dreyfuss,

1986). So, too, is this true for the creative curriculum leader involved in the details of each day at work.

It is a reality of our age that there is a scarcity of resources. The curriculum leader is expected to allocate such resources wisely. This quite simply means that priorities must be set. The curriculum leader continually asks himself or herself, "What do I value more than something else?" It is helpful to identify one's own values in a general or abstract way, but one quickly discovers that it is the specific content of one's values, and the contingency of variables, that are the critical matter with respect to priority setting.

For example, in one elementary school, teachers and students in a wing of the school were continually cold due to a faulty heating system. The Site Based Management committee, strongly supported by the rhetoric of the principal, pressured the principal to do something about this matter. The principal worked through channels, but in the meantime that wing of the building remained cold. The SBM committee, taking the principal and the superintendent of schools at their word on the value of shared decision making, wrote a memorandum to the board of education, giving specifics about the heating problem. The superintendent of schools was irate, but the principal "walked his talk" and supported the SBM committee and the faculty they represented.

A second example involves a proactive teacher, Judy, who wishes to initiate a curriculum-planning project in a school system whose superintendent is unwilling to commit many resources to any project that leaves him off the steering committee. Judy faces a dilemma: A basic tenet of the project is local control with power primarily in the hands of team leaders in each school, but the superintendent feels threatened by this tenet unless his presence on the steering committee is a reality. Judy will need to set priorities within the context of these realities in order to achieve as many of the goals and objectives as possible.

If Judy decides to invite the superintendent to be a member of the steering committee, she will probably receive more resources for her project, which will help persons at the local level feel more relaxed about what can be done. (They won't have to worry about phone bills, supplies, secretarial support, and the like.) At the same time,

Judy will risk having the superintendent exert his positional authority on the project, which will be a threat to local control.

Let us imagine that Judy decides not to invite the superintendent
to be a member of the steering committee, so resources for the
project are severely limited. The result may well be a kind of bureaucratic monitoring of the use of limited resources, with persons at the
local level tense about what can be done. (Approval forms will have
to be filled out for the use of the telephone, the acquisition of
materials, travel money, and the like, with little hope of receiving
many of these resources.)

In the first instance, where the superintendent is formally involved and resources are plentiful, general goals will be empha-
sized, with trust given to persons expected to reach these more
general curriculum-planning ends. In the second instance, where
resources are scarce, greater emphasis will probably be given to
behavioral objectives since administrators will probably be nervous
about not going over the budget. A lack of trust will therefore be
communicated to project members. The monitoring of the budget
will create the kind of bureaucratic central control that Judy origi-
nally intended to avoid.

In effect, Judy's decision to include or not include the superintendent can lead to a similar result. She must decide which decision
will probably be least likely to threaten her original goal of giving
local control to project members. In short, she will set priorities in
accordance with her vision for the project.

The History of the Setting

Setting is a term or concept that may be useful to the creative
curriculum leader. A setting is "any instance when two or more
people come together in new and sustained relationships to achieve
common goals" (Sarason, 1972, p. ix). Examples of settings are: a
classroom in the fall of the year; a new organization for principals
in the state; and the formation of a Site-Based Management team in
a school. When a new setting is created, it of necessity encounters
the history of a previous setting.

Creative curriculum leaders avoid giving attention to the history of the setting at their own peril. Yet, curriculum leaders are tempted to act as if life began with the first day they entered the setting, or began creating the setting. Such a position flatters the leader's ego and makes no demands on him or her to systematically study "before the beginning" influences (Sarason, 1972). A dramatic representation of this took place at our home a few years ago. A guest arrived at the front door 2 hours after a party began and said, "Oh, the party has just begun, huh?" I responded, "No, it looks that way to you since you just got here." (Have you ever had this feeling about the behavior of a new principal or superintendent of schools?)

The challenge to the creative curriculum leader interested in creating a setting is to relate to the setting's zeitgeist or "what's in the air, and what is in the air derives from the existing social structure" (Sarason, 1972, p. 25). More specifically, the curriculum leader needs to understand *ways of thinking* (assumptions and conceptions) different from his or her own ways of thinking (Sarason, 1972). Why is this? It is simply because the new setting proposed by the curriculum leader "confronts a preexisting complicated structure of relationships, parts of which work against and parts that work for the creation of a new setting" (Sarason, 1972, p. 42).

The following questions may be helpful to the curriculum leader in relating to the history of the setting (Sarason, 1972).

Is the need for a new setting clearly recognized by a substantial element of the old setting? If the answer to this question is yes, the curriculum leader is more likely to be invited to introduce changes in the old setting. If the answer is no, the curriculum leader may well be considered a troublemaker who wants to disrupt routines that have provided comfort and security to those in the old setting.

Was the need for a new setting openly voiced and therefore initiated by those within the old setting? In the previous question the keyword was *recognized*, but in the present question the keywords are *openly voiced* and *initiated*. If the members of the old setting reached the point where they openly voiced their need for a new setting, they probably ran some risk in doing so. If they actually initiated a new setting while being part of the old setting, they clearly bought into the change process. (In many settings, unhappy persons are passively aggressive: They don't help those who wish to perpetuate the old setting; neither do they openly challenge such persons, but rather they undercut their efforts.) The curriculum leader needs to identify key persons who have given resources to openly voicing the need for a new setting and taking action in order to initiate the construction of a new setting.

Our experience is that the chances of success in creating a new setting are greatly enhanced if the need for a new setting is clearly recognized and voiced by key leaders in the old setting, and if such persons initiate action in behalf of the creation of a new setting. Persons in settings frequently say that they see no need for changes. Furthermore, they add, they are tired of "outsiders" coming in and trying to introduce things without asking whether people in the setting want such changes.

Do those who initiated the drive toward the creation of a new setting recognize the importance of understanding the history of the setting? If not, they run the risk of counterforces that they never anticipated. A department chairperson in a high school wanted to create a new setting involving her seven-member staff. Carried away with her enthusiasm for the new setting, she failed to discover that most staff members were secure in their bureaucratic relationship with the previous chairperson. The less authoritarian, shared decision-making plan she wanted to initiate was considered a threat, so the new setting had little chance for survival.

Are those interested in creating a new setting clear as to their goals and objectives as well as the predominant goals and objectives held by members of the old setting? Sometimes a person's enthusiasm for the new setting prompts him or her to give attention to activities, with goals and objectives neglected. Total attention to activities can lead to an interesting carnival atmosphere, in which events have no common threads or directions. In short, there is no meaning for the curriculum program or project. Curriculum planners sometimes encounter such a situation, whereby subgroups occupy themselves with activities but the total group seems to lack rationale for its existence.

Do members of the old setting recognize that persons generally have unlimited desires, but the setting has limited resources? The curriculum leader will sometimes find that members of the old setting who want changes believe that just wanting such changes will bring

them about. Such persons haven't squarely faced the fact that resources are always limited, and enthusiasm for change isn't enough
in itself. (How difficult is it for a honeymoon couple to sit down
before the honeymoon and discuss what they might not be able to
do because of limited resources?)

*Is the rhetoric of those in the old setting consistent with the degree of
commitment they exhibit in their actions?* The curriculum leader will
sometimes encounter persons in the old setting whose rhetoric
outdistances their commitment to action. A physically active teacher
polled faculty members throughout the school to find out if they
were interested in becoming corporate members of a nearby athletic
club. Since only 15 responses were needed to buy such a member-
ship, the teacher was happily surprised by the 30 potential members
who signed forms. A month later, when dues were supposed to be
sent to the athletic club, only 5 of the 30 had sent in their member-
ship fees. The initial reaction of the teacher who initiated action was
one of bitterness. "Never again," he moaned.

*What kinds of covenants have members of the old setting formed, and
what kinds do they say they would like to have in the future?* Using the
covenant formation framework in an earlier part of this chapter, the
curriculum leader can construct a profile of the old setting by noting
the kinds of covenants already formed. An early diagnosis of possible future relationships can also be made as the curriculum leader
converses with members of the old setting about relationships they
would like to have in the future.

*Do leaders who are interested in creating a new setting see their role as
a matter of chance, or as part of the natural history of events?* The
emergence of leadership at a particular time in a setting's history is
part of the natural evolution of that setting, and yet many leaders
fail to see this. Rather, they consider it a matter of chance. The
curriculum leader needs to identify and analyze those forces that
brought him or her to power at this time in the history of the setting.

*Do leaders who wish to create a new setting act as if all members of the
old setting want to be invited to play some role in the creation of the new
setting?* The curriculum leader interested in creating a new setting
may be enticed to think that all members of the old setting don't
want to be (or shouldn't be) invited to join in creating the new
setting, but in fact all are flattered by the invitation, regardless of

whether they make this known publicly. The challenge to the curriculum leader is to find appropriate and sometimes subtle ways to involve all members in creating the new setting. In this way they assume ownership for the creation of the new setting. Meeting this challenge is consistent with the definition of creative leadership: using your talents to help others identify and use their talents.

Do members of the old setting who plan to give leadership to the new setting understand the setting's concept, or do they view changes in narrower terms—such as a series of discrete decisions and actions? It is important that all who will give leadership in creating a new setting share a common view of the context or framework in which change will take place. The setting's concept provides leaders with such a framework. The curriculum leader will probably encounter many members of the old setting who see change as a series of discrete and often unrelated events.

Do members of the old setting who plan to give leadership to the creation of the new setting think in extreme terms, or do they make finer distinctions? It is easy for persons involved in creating something "new" to think in terms of the good people (those who want to create a new setting) and the bad people (those who oppose the creation of a new setting). In order to be an effective curriculum leader, one must make finer distinctions that will invite people with many shades of opinions, especially the dissident voice, into the creation process.

In conclusion, the curriculum leader involved in the creation process of a setting is creatively challenged to consider past events, trends, and leadership patterns formed prior to his or her entrance into the setting. This challenge to the artistry of the creative curriculum leader is what brings life to those who are willing to meet it.

The Culture of the Setting

The history of the setting may be defined as "the way we *did* things around here." The culture of the setting is "the way we *do* things around here." The basic values of a setting are expressed in its way of life or culture. The creative curriculum leader must consider the culture of a setting, for a culture's imperatives or "commands" will surely influence what is possible to achieve. A few examples of cultural imperatives follow:

1. All buildings have heavy screens to protect windows from vandalism.
2. Doors to bathrooms are locked between classes to curtail vandalism and physical assaults.
3. All buildings have traditional architecture (for example, 90-degree corners).
4. Adults stand up much of the day, whereas students sit behind desks in most classes, desks that are smaller than those used by adults.
5. Adults ask most of the questions, and students are expected to provide most of the answers.

This brief list of five existing regularities in a particular school setting points out the distance required in order to identify cultural imperatives. Seymour Sarason, Professor Emeritus of Psychology at Yale University, urges us to imagine that we are from outer space, with our space platform directly above the institution being studied (1971).

Three concepts are useful to us as we distance ourselves from the culture of a setting in order to better understand it: symbols, rituals, and myths.

Symbols are concrete expressions of more abstract ideas. A symbol quickly conveys a whole set of emotions. The lectern, for example, symbolizes the positional authority of the teacher. A physical education teacher's warmup outfit symbolizes an informal leadership style, but the whistle around the physical education teacher's neck symbolizes positional authority of a more formal nature. Common language expressions in a setting also tell us about the culture of the setting. The language used by school psychologists, for example, is quite different from the language used by classroom teachers.

Rituals emerge from human interactions in order to provide persons with the emotional security associated with predictable behavior. Attendance taking, flag ceremonies, and furniture arrangements serve as examples of rituals in settings. It is inevitable that rituals will emerge in a setting. The curriculum leader can evaluate a setting, using rituals as an indicator of regularities in the setting's culture. The curriculum leader is in the position of introducing new rituals in a setting. For example, a new high school principal decided to hold monthly faculty meetings in classroom areas of each department. Each department introduced the faculty meeting with a brief description of its activities.

Myths are "stories" persons in a setting create in order to explain the unexplainable. These myths help the person manipulate tensions about interpersonal relationships. They contain elements of reality and unreality, as demonstrated by the commonly held myth that "the boss controls everyone in the setting." If we study the setting carefully we find that there are many and diverse ways, some ingenious, for getting bosses to do what others want them to do. For example, in one school system where the superintendent prided himself on curriculum leadership, as symbolized by his attendance at curriculum conferences, central office leaders and others used their informal sources of power to influence what conferences the superintendent attended. They prided themselves on their use of such influence.

Finally, the "know thyself" theme of this book, a theme originated in the immortal words of Socrates, is directly related to symbols, rituals, and myths. They are models or constructs we use to create ourselves (May, 1975). Symbols and myths are embodied in ritual. It is not only useful to each of us to know this as a personal life script is acted out, but it is also invaluable to observe and make sense out of the lives of others as they do likewise. The creative curriculum leader's actions set the tone for the culture of the organization she leads. "Whether she likes it or not," according to M. Scott Peck (1993), "her personality will become a template for the school, the department, the hospital, the corporation, or the entire business she manages" (p. 258). Once again, for those you lead, you will be the curriculum.

Sources of Power

In using our talents to help others identify and use their talents, we draw on several sources of power. In discussing these sources of power, we will see how our society's view of them has changed.

Positional authority is power by virtue of one's position in the organization. It is commonly associated with bureaucratic forms of organization, for those with more positional authority give "commands" to their subordinates who have less. Regardless of the respect, or lack of it, accorded the person with positional authority, the bureaucratic subordinate is expected to obey such commands. Traditionally, it has been drawn upon heavily, but observers in the area of leadership education argue that drawing upon positional authority is much like using a battery: The more you use it the less there is to use in the future. They therefore recommend that positional authority should be suspended by the leader whenever possible.

Expertise is a source of power attributed to persons because of their recognized ability to do something well. A curriculum leader in a school may, for example, be recognized as a well-organized person who has demonstrated expertise in writing reports. She is therefore asked to head the accreditation planning team for the school. The ability to organize and articulate ideas is a very important kind of expertise essential to the curriculum leadership process.

Succorance is an informal kind of power that leaves others with the feeling that they are supported emotionally. It is commonly associated with counseling and coaching. "You can do it" is the message transmitted. Curriculum leaders often reach the place in the curriculum-planning process where they are ready to give up, due to a lack of interest on the part of committee members or opposition from a person or group. It is precisely at this point that succorance can give momentum to tasks that must be completed. The morale of the group depends on this kind of support.

Charisma is a sort of magnetic charm often equated with sex appeal. Nonverbal messages, such as smiles and nods of approval, are the vehicles of communication used by the charismatic leader. Style of dress and the leader's bearing give added charisma.

The creative curriculum leader integrates the sources of power in a manner appropriate for a particular situation. This integration is based on a realistic assessment of the leader's talents, as well as the talents of fellow team members.

Societal changes in the way we view the sources of power were brought home to me by the story of a 40-year-old teacher, whose mother still lives in the mountains of North Carolina:

Our family doctor in the mountains told my mother that she must immediately prepare herself psychologically and physically for surgery in order to amputate a leg ravaged by sugar diabetes. The general practitioner added that her other leg would also have to be amputated in due time. Our family had always trusted the professional judgment of this physician because of his position of authority. My mother prepared herself for surgery. It just didn't seem right to me, however, and so I talked her into going with me to Winston-Salem, North Carolina, a 2-hour drive from our home that we almost never made when we were children. A specialist at Wake Forest's Bowman Gray School of Medicine said that amputation was not necessary, given newly found ways of treating diabetes. My mother has been walking around well for 15 years on legs our family doctor was preparing to remove.

The story graphically depicts the tremendous changes our society has undergone in relation to the role of positional authority. The creative curriculum leader is challenged by such changes to a new kind of artistry in leading others and knowing more about self.

The Aesthetics of Creating a Setting

Throughout our discussion of the creative curriculum leader's challenge in creating new settings, references have been made to the artistry of creative curriculum leadership. One sometimes gets the feeling that using one's talents to help others identify and use their talents is much like being a leader of a symphony orchestra. The conductor is not an expert on each instrument, but must use artistry to bring out such expertise in orchestra members.

The title of this section of the chapter, "The Aesthetics of Creating a Setting," intimates a process or "in movement" orientation, rather than a product orientation. A more product-oriented title might have been "The Aesthetics of a Created Setting."

A product, such as a curriculum report or a slide presentation of an experimental project, is a tangible or concrete expression of a process. Its concreteness makes it a powerful political symbol of progress. Administrators can show off this product as an example of tax money wisely spent or leadership effectively exerted. ("Remember," one wag said, "you can accomplish anything if you let the boss get the credit.")

A product is summative—a completed end or result that can be evaluated. Process, on the other hand, is formative. It is not what has been done, but instead what is unfolding or becoming. Those who argue that the purpose of education is to produce people who produce things are uncomfortable with the idea that the purpose of education is to help persons who are in the process of becoming what they can be in relating to self, others, and the environment. Philosopher Martin Buber (1970) refers to this as the difference between the I-It relationship and the I-Thou relationship. Although persons' relationships with things are important, they are (should be) less important than persons' relationships with others and oneself (1970). Products, the fruit of our labor, should not be denigrated, for they are benchmarks that tell us something of our progress, and their relative permanence lends itself to evaluation, pride, and a sense of efficacy.

Process gives us a sense of the fluidity of life's forces. These forces are always changing and challenging us to change. They encourage us to have a growing edge, which in turn serves as an incentive for further growth and development. The growing edge may be referred to as reconceptualization, for in the process of creating a setting, we learn to see the familiar in unfamiliar ways and the unfamiliar in familiar ways. On the one hand, the curriculum leader involved in the aesthetic process of creating a setting moves into the actor role, and it is in this role that he or she views members of the setting and the environment in different ways. (It is as if someone who has repeatedly sat in the back of an auditorium suddenly decides to sit in the front row.) At the same time, the curriculum leader involved in the aesthetic process of creating a setting perceives familiar happenings, such as traditional arrangements of furniture in meetings, in different ways; the leader now has the power to change such arrangements and set the stage for important committee decisions. The main benefit of being a proactive leader is that you can make things happen.

A second dimension of the aesthetics of creating a setting, one that complements emphasis on process, is that of giving attention to oneself. Those who only give attention to helping others learn not to relate to their own feelings of doubt, joy, pain, and ecstasy. Rather, such persons project their own values and beliefs on others, without really understanding the feelings of either those being helped or themselves.

Seymour Sarason, who has written so much and so well about the creation of settings, relates that he and his colleagues chose to create meaning and pleasure for themselves as they created the Yale Psycho-Educational Clinic: "We were going to judge ourselves only second-arily by how helpful we were to others. Conceivably we would not be very helpful, and conceivably we might even be harmful and yet be successful in terms of personal learning and growth" (1972, p. 116).

It could be argued that Sarason and associates increased the likelihood of success for all in the clinic because of their interest in personal learning and growth—an interest that must have been stimulating to others. After, all, it can be argued that one must simply get at a high level in order to give at a high level (Sarason, 1971). And they demonstrated their willingness to make themselves vulnerable by having the courage to risk failure.

Giving attention to oneself is part of a third dimension of the aesthetics of creating a setting—priority setting. Those who give attention to the creation of settings quickly realize that clients in a setting are less a creation of leaders in the setting than of the setting itself. For example, the child in a classroom responds to something larger than the teacher—namely, the setting, which has its own life. Recognizing this helps curriculum leaders give first priority to the entire setting as an influencing body. How strange it sometimes seems that the rhetoric in our folklore and myths in education leads us to believe that one person as leader, such as the principal, teacher, or chief administrator, makes all the difference in relating to the client. In fact, the personality of the setting is usually more powerful than the personality of the individual.

Part of priority setting is realizing that a leader involved in creating a setting can't reach everyone in an effective way. One is reminded of the statement of an administrator who gave the com-mencement address to graduating physicians: Eighty percent of those patients who come to your office will be fine, regardless of what you do; 10 percent are terminally ill and you should do whatever possible to make their last days comfortable ones; and 10 percent need critical diagnosis, for their welfare depends on you as a physician; the difficulty is in knowing which patient falls into which group. Indeed, this is a difficulty, but knowing that you, the curriculum leader, are not and cannot be the be-all and end-all for each person in the setting removes a heavy burden—a self-imposed one—from your shoulders. You will not have to pretend to yourself and others that you are a superman or superwoman.

Emphasis on self-understanding and growth in the creation of settings process should not be taken to mean selfishness. The curriculum leader's relationships with others—the consequences of leadership—are an important aspect of the aesthetics of creating a setting. The attention we have given to kinds of covenants and duration of covenants was meant to convey the importance of social intercourse. The elements of trust, autonomy, and initiative are positive results of rich and varied social intercourse.

A sense of playfulness is another dimension of the aesthetics of creating a setting. The curriculum leader as artist will convey the same kind of zestiness that an artist communicates through art forms such as paintings, music, and drama (Brubaker, 1979). Unfortunately, our culture has "commanded" us to view work and play as discrete processes, as evidenced in our language: workbooks, playgrounds, work areas, play areas, and the like. The curriculum leader as a creator of settings will thoroughly immerse self in the creative process, so that work and play are integrated. Any distinction between them will become blurred.

As stated earlier in this book, there seems to be a real hunger on the part of educators in a technical society for the openness and just plain fun we often experienced as children (Brubaker, 1992). This was brought to my attention recently in a conversation with a superintendent of schools in a large school system. Our time together began as a ritual in which we talked about something outside of ourselves—tasks that needed to be performed so that the staff development experiences being planned would be successful. As is often the case with such rituals, the tone of the exchange was polite, businesslike, and rather bland. Near the end of the conversation the superintendent came to life and said:

You know what really amazes me when I think about where I might go with the remainder of my career and try to be more self-actualized? I wonder how all of this happened. As I look back at my quick moves from teacher to assistant principal to principal to superintendent in three schools systems and think about my humble beginnings, I ask myself, "How did all of this happen?"

The first thing I noted about the superintendent's comments was that they were driven by a sense of awe, wonder, and amazement (Fox, 1983). His imagination and playfulness were evident in his eyes, an intensity of voice, and a forward movement of his head. His total being said, "I am alive with this challenge." As Robert Bly points out, "If we choose 'the one precious thing' . . . the inner King in us that has been asleep for so many years wakes up" (Bly, 1990, p. 177). The superintendent didn't say, "I have a problem, and what is the most efficient way to solve it?" He embraced the mystery of his upward mobility and wanted to understand it. He didn't engage himself in compulsive busyness, often designed to eliminate or set aside awe, wonder, and amazement. It was as if he had stopped the elevator at one of the upper-level floors, looked out the window, and saw a garden. He wanted to make sense out of how he got to this floor and he wondered what it would be like to spend more time tending the garden. (*Self-actualization* was the term he used to identify the garden.)

The lesson for us as creative curriculum leaders interested in the aesthetics of creating settings is obvious: Use the celebration of the creative process as a starting point. As William James expressed it, "Man's chief difference from the brutes lies in the exuberant excess of his subjective propensities. . . . Prune down his extravagances, sober him, and you undo him" (James, 1979, p. 224).

It is hoped that our discussion of the aesthetics of creating a setting will stimulate you to think about the challenge in this area to you as a creative curriculum leader. In the process you will probably be led into the humanities, such as art, music, drama, and dance. It will be your challenge to integrate the spirit of the artist with the spirit of the scientist, for such an integration is essential for creative curriculum leadership in the 21st century. M. Scott Peck (1993) captures this integration in his own leadership experience:

> I keep referring to the integration of task and process as an art as well as a skill. Should you ever have the opportunity to observe a mature community doing it even relatively well, not only will you see civility or organizational behavior in its highest form but you will also witness a human phenomenon of great beauty. (p. 344)

Conclusion

Creative curriculum leadership is more difficult and challenging than top-down manipulative leadership that in effect uses others for the gains of the person in the higher position of authority. The main payoff, however, for the creative curriculum leader and others is the sense of curiosity, awe, wonder, and amazement associated with the learning process. In short, the leader as learner makes all of the difference in creating community.

Case 9: Your Response to a Speech by a Feminist Educator

You are a second-year teacher whose relationship with your teaching mentor can best be described as excellent. You are like-minded on important views of teaching and social issues in general. As luck would have it, both of you are seeking jobs for the following year and think it would be great if you could find jobs in the same school.

You and your mentor decide to visit a nearby university to hear an educator's feminist critique of schools and schooling. The feminist speaker begins by saying that it is generally acknowledged that teaching is a feminized profession, whereas educational administration is not. In effect, the feminist continues, this places positional authority in schools and school systems in the hands of men. It does not make sense, according to the feminist speaker, to add on the feminist perspective, for in effect this simply reinforces the masculine industrial-age metaphor of the man in the driver's seat. Subject matter within disciplines, educational and occupational hierarchies with their sexual division of labor (men in administration and women in teaching), and other male-dominated mechanisms supporting the status quo are the result of adding on the feminist critique, rather than starting afresh with a very new view as to what schools and schooling can and should be. The feminist speaker concludes by saying that all of you, men and women, who support the status quo will relegate women to the same role that nurses have played in relation to doctors, and in the process both women and men will be dehumanized.

The speaker, a very bright, dynamic, and articulate person, has given you and your cooperating teacher plenty to think about. What will your reaction be as you search for a teaching position, and what will your advice be to your mentor? Please choose the best of the following alternatives:

1. You and your friend should seek a school with a principal, male or female, who has a similar view of what is wrong with schools and schooling and what needs to be done to make things right.
2. Choose a school whose principal is a good leader and manager without regard to his or her view with regard to feminism.

Case 9: Rationales for the Alternative Responses

1. The first thing you should do is to give thanks for a genuine friendship. You have established a covenant that is both long-lasting and intense. Such relationships are rare in today's world and can lead to high quality of life at home and at school. The issue of relations between genders in regard to leadership is a highly significant one and should be a major consideration in your choice of a school and its principal. To not give attention to this issue is to bury your head in the sand. Do your homework and find a principal who will set the tone for the school's culture in a morally responsible way. This is probably the best answer.

2. It is indeed wise to value your good relationship with your friend and mentor, for such covenants are indeed rare. But the

principal's role is almost completely that of a manager. It is important that you and your friend have a school that runs smoothly. Issues, such as relations between genders, are of little consequence compared to effective teaching. The problem with this response is that the role of principal is defined in a purely technical way, without regard to value and moral dimensions. How can you teach democracy without giving attention to such dimensions? Consider a better response.

Case 10: A Site-Based Management Proposal

Your school year begins with a 3-day retreat. Principals in the school system recently attended a conference on Site-Based Management (SBM). They agreed that each school in the system should be invited to apply for pilot or experimental status in moving to a SBM model.

Some reservations are raised about SBM at the conference, although all agree that there are drawbacks with the traditional top-down way of exercising authority in organizations in a new information age society. And all agree that facilitative power has real potential for professional decision making on the part of teachers and administrators. Facilitative power, according to one principal at the conference, is one way to overcome both obvious and not so obvious areas of disagreement in the school. (By facilitative power, it is meant that you bring out the leadership qualities of others, rather than giving them "commands.")

The main drawback discussed at the conference is that some principals can misuse SBM. Specifically, a principal can blame SBM committee members for his or her own mistakes. And it is also true that ultimately the principal at each school is the formally designated leader who is responsible for the school.

What will your reaction be to the invitation to have your school become a pilot project for SBM? Please choose the best of the following options:

1. Give leadership to not supporting SBM in your school.
2. Give leadership to supporting SBM in your school.
3. Let things take their course. Either way is fine.

Case 10: Rationales for
the Alternative Responses

1. Shared decision making, the essence of the SBM model, is a misnomer. There is always one formally designated leader in the school—the principal. And if he or she is expected to suspend his or her positional authority, that positional authority can always be returned at a moment's notice. All committees in a school are simply advisory, with real power in the hands of the principal. To pretend otherwise is deceitful. A weak principal can forget his or her role, and the faculty and perhaps the students can take over the school. Chaos will then reign. Be wary of mechanisms that quickly promise change. The quick fix doesn't work. Also, if SBM is put in place, faculty will be expected to enter into an intense and long-range covenant with one another and the principal. You are hired to teach, not administer the school. All of these arguments hold in some schools where SBM has been misused. However, if your school has teachers with leadership potential and interest in shared decision making, SBM has real potential. To reject the proposal out-of-hand for a pilot project is a mistake. Consider other alternatives.

2. The invitation to apply for pilot status in the new SBM program has tremendous potential for effecting change in the school. Facilitative power is clearly consistent with societal changes in general, and the move from an industrial age to an information age society in particular. It is also a sign of hope that professionalism can be enhanced and a sense of community can be increased in the school. This does mean the probability of an intense covenant of considerable duration, but the payoff can be significant. You must be alert, however, to the possibility that the principal, who is formally designated as the final authority in the school, can take back at any moment power shared with teachers. If such an event occurs, you and your colleagues must know how to use other sources of power to achieve your goals. In conclusion, there is the real possibility of creating a Win/Win climate in your school. Go for it.

3. There are advantages to not getting involved. You won't be blamed if things go wrong, and you can hang around the edges, thus saving your resources, such as time, energy, and expertise. However, the move toward SBM has gone too far to simply play a passive

role. This Win/Win or No Deal way of relating to colleagues and the principal will in effect keep you out of the school arena. You will not accept your professional responsibility by taking this stance and you could well convey the feeling that you are either uninterested or too good to get involved. Seek a better response.

Case 11: Testing Irregularities
Are Reported to You

You are a respected educator in a medium-size school system. You have received a letter from a parent volunteer who spends a good deal of time in an elementary school. The letter contains the following comments:

There has been a good deal of coverage of testing irregularities (cheating) on television (such as "60 Minutes") and in newspapers.

Since I love my job as a parent volunteer, I must remain anonymous and trust you to assure this. However, I have been an actual witness to these things as teachers have given the C.A.T. (California Achievement Test):

1. Stopping mid-test to teach something coming up on the test that the students had not been taught

2. Before handing in the tests given that day, looking ahead to copy down the upcoming test questions and teaching them verbatim

3. Tapping a child on the shoulder to point out an incorrect answer and giving him the A-OK sign when he erased it and filled in the correct answer

4. Going overtime

5. Allowing children to go back and finish up previous sections that they had not completed within the time limit

6. Reading the directions more than once to the children or paraphrasing them to emphasize what the teacher especially wanted the children to know

7. Allowing the children to have little math-fact cheat cards in their desks that they could refer to during the test, since they never learned math facts on their own

What will you do? Please choose the best of the following alternatives:

1. Share the letter with the proper authorities in the school system.
2. Share the letter with the proper authorities in the school system and follow up to be sure that action has been taken.
3. Ignore the letter.

Case 11: Rationales for the Alternative Responses

1. Cheating cannot be condoned, but must be put in the context of modern society. Unrelenting emphasis on high achievement test scores has reached epidemic proportions, with cheating the natural result. Our society has supported the Win/Lose norm, with many parents doing whatever is necessary for their children to get special advantage over other children. Assigned readings are stolen from university libraries so that pre-med and pre-law students get higher grades that will give them special advantage to get into medical and law schools. Many parents pressure their children to learn to read before they reach kindergarten. Some parents do whatever is necessary to give their children special advantage in becoming members of cheerleading and athletic teams. Cheating is not only wrong but also contaminates test score results of students who have done well on tests without cheating. Share the letter with proper authorities in your school system. All of the above is true, but stops short of informing you as to what will happen, if anything, once the letter has been shared with authorities. Search for a better alternative.

2. The response to this matter described in number 1 above is necessary but insufficient. The issues raised by the letter are so important that you must not only report the matter to authorities, such as the director of testing and the superintendent(s), but also be sure that appropriate action is taken, including the retesting of the classes involved and appropriate punishment of the culpable teachers. You may well experience some difficulties and pain as you give resources to this matter, but the issues involved are significant enough to endure a high level of commitment.

3. Not getting involved will conserve your resources in the short run. However, you will not be meeting your professional responsibilities by hiding your head in the sand. Find a better response.

Case 12: New Principal
States Intention to Ignore
History and Culture of the School

Recent years have been very difficult for you in your school. The recently released principal had a leadership style that divided the faculty on a number of key issues. As a result, the superintendent of schools has recommended and the board of education has appointed a new principal from another state.

During the fall orientation meeting of the faculty, the new principal says the following: "It is time for a fresh start for all of us in this school. I don't want any of you to come to me with stories about past difficulties. Let us begin as if this is a brand-new school with brand-new faculty members."

What will you do in reaction to the new principal's comments? Please choose the best of the following alternatives:

1. Ignore the new principal's comments.
2. Remind yourself that the history and culture of the school are a significant variable in decision making at the present time, and make this known to the faculty and principal at the orientation meeting for the faculty.
3. The history and culture of the school are important to keep in mind as present decisions are made. However, you must find a better time—probably in a private conversation with the principal—to share your view with the principal.

Case 12: Rationales for
the Alternative Responses

1. Once again, to ignore the matter will conserve your resources in the short run and keep you out of trouble. However, the new principal's position is important enough so that you will not be meeting your professional responsibilities by doing nothing. Choose a better option.

2. You are right to give attention to the history and culture of the setting. And to address this matter directly, at the front end of your relationship with the new principal, he or she and the faculty will know that you are willing to act out your beliefs. The difficulty with this response is that the new principal is trying to establish his or her credibility with the faculty for the first time in an official set-ting—the first faculty meeting. Your outspoken action will leave him or her little room to save face. Seek a better alternative.

3. Some action on your part needs to be taken. The history and culture of the setting must be taken into account by your new principal and other school leaders in the decision-making process. The best time to deal with this issue is in a one-to-one conversation with the new principal. You will not be openly challenging the new principal in a formal setting this way.

7

Civility in Leadership
The Ultimate Difference

Civility is hardly the only way to live, but it is the only way that is worthwhile.

M. Scott Peck (1993, p. 54)

ffective citizenship has been a major goal of public education in the United States since its inception (Brubaker,
1967). The teaching of "civics" was viewed as the mechanism for
inculcating proper values in the young. The very health of democratic society was perceived to be at stake as schools geared up to
meet this challenge. Public commitment is evidenced by self-
imposed taxation. The word *civility* sounds much like civics, with
the former usually linked to manners and politeness, those small
behaviors that tend to make others like us (Peck, 1993). However,
the civil leader sometimes does things that don't win the approval
of others. M. Scott Peck refers to an amusing but profound quote
from Oliver Herford: "A gentleman is one who never hurts anyone's
feelings unintentionally" (Peck, 1993). In other words, manners
and politeness are moral behaviors if they increase our consciousness of the preciousness of each person and the relationship of self,
others, and organizations on behalf of this humanistic tradition
(Peck, 1993).

When manners and politeness are invoked to simply get the approval of others, they are self-serving and as such usually don't have the ring of authenticity and integrity. When manners and politeness are used in this way, they communicate the leader's desire to avoid all pain, and yet the health of a person or organization is often a painful process (Peck, 1993).

An example of pain that often accompanies civility is described best by a third-grade teacher who has recently been losing sleep and weight:

> Each school in our system has a "report card" that tells the public our annual goal, objectives, and plan of action. Our school's major goal was to raise standardized test scores. My class was well on its way to meeting this goal when a new student, a nonreader with low test scores, arrived on the scene from another town. My first reaction was "Why did I have to get this student? I wish he would move again!" At the same time I realized that I, a good teacher, was exactly the kind of person who could make a difference in his life. (Brubaker & Simon, 1993, p. 19)

How did the third-grade teacher reconcile this contradiction? First, she was conscious of the pain she was experiencing and recognized that her devotion to a "higher authority" than self—the preciousness of the child—was more important than appearing to be a winner with higher test scores. Second, she decided to do the work necessary to deal with this situation, rather than denying its reality. Without being conscious of it, she located her commitment to the child and situation at Level 5, and perhaps Level 4, on the following Commitment Scale/Hierarchy (Brubaker & Nelson, 1974, p. 102):

1. I will sacrifice my life and/or the lives of my family and/or those I dearly love.
2. I will give up the respect of those whom I love and I'll forego my status and professional achievement.
3. I will forego economic security and my career.
4. I will have serious conflicts between what I think should be done and my reluctance to do it. I may have to alter my work

style and give up those techniques which had previously been successful and beneficial and learn new ones.

5. I will have to alter some habits with which I'm quite comfortable, thus making my job somewhat more difficult. I will feel uncomfortable from time to time as I'll do things that don't seem to be the best way to do them based on my past experience and present assumptions.

6. It doesn't make any difference as past experience indicates. My choice, therefore, is between Tweedledee and Tweedledum.

Did the teacher know that she would intentionally hurt the feelings of the principal, superintendent of schools, and school board? Yes. Her actions were conscious and deliberative. But, she was simply committed to a lateral rather than a hierarchical relationship with her organization—the school and the school system (Peck, 1993). She had made a civil commitment in response to an incivility—pressure to achieve high test scores so that adult educators would appear to be winners. In fact, we could well say that her bias for children worked in her favor. William Buckley (1982) underscores how bias can be a kind of advantage: "Ken Galbraith and I have in common what strikes some as a disadvantage, but isn't: namely our plainspoken bias, which gives a harnessing energy to our work" (p. 239).

A second example relates to my moving to the South more than 20 years ago. A colleague who had lived in the state all of his life counseled me on one of the major civilities of the region: "We don't go anywhere where we aren't wanted." I asked him about the *civil* rights sit-ins that had occurred in Greensboro, but heard a reply that demonstrated no connection between *civil* rights and African-American students not served at the lunch counter. The sit-ins literally placed themselves at Level 1 of the Commitment Scale/Hierarchy in defiance of traditional Southern manners and politeness.

Perhaps the main benefit in exercising your civil rights is to yourself. In February 1986, Anatoli Shcharansky (1986)—Soviet Jew, dissident, and accused American spy—was released from a Soviet prison to Israel, and freedom, after 9 years in custody. His weight had varied from 81 to 165 pounds. He had become not only a powerful voice of dissent in the Soviet Union but also a bridge between Soviet Jewry and the rest of the human rights movement. When he was asked about his time in prison, he responded as follows:

> You are punished if you write to the authorities on behalf of another prisoner—say a sick man who is not getting any medical attention. The authorities say, "Look, your letters don't help." And they are logically right. But there exists another, inner logic: the prisoner who writes such a letter may not save his neighbor in the next cell, but he saves his soul. (p. 38)

A Metaphor for Schools

It is interesting to hear school administrators and teachers use metaphors to describe their schools. The most frequently used metaphor is that of the family. As M. Scott Peck (1993) has noted, the primary role of a family is to nurture its members. And it is true that nurturing is a major role of effective principals and assistant principals. Yet the family metaphor doesn't hold in other respects. For example, principals hire and fire teachers and other staff members. These functions are more accurately associated with a business. In Robert Frost's poem, "The Death of the Hired Man," the husband, who is a farmer, says, "Home is the place where, when you have to go there, they have to take you in" (Peck, 1993, p. 196).

Another difficulty with the family metaphor for schools is that it is easy to conceive of them as patriarchies or matriarchies, where the principal is in effect a benevolent or not so benevolent parent. Teachers and other staff members can, through transference, a "neurotic and uncivil distortion of reality," continue to relate to their new "father" or "mother" in positive or negative ways (Peck, 1993, p. 214).

In recent years, a more apt metaphor for a school is that of a business. Test scores and other number-related products are marketed by some teachers, principals, superintendents, and school board members (Peck, 1993). Testing irregularities, an euphemism for cheating, are a side effect as teachers and administrators want to appear to be winners. In some cases teachers and others are given permission to cheat. In other cases administrators are so focused on raising test scores that they simply don't give attention to testing irregularities.

At any rate, the creative curriculum leader can use the concept of metaphors as a way to discuss with teachers and others which metaphors promote true civility and which don't. There is obviously no one right answer to this question.

The Table Manners of Leadership
and Developing Your Own Curriculum

When I was a child I was asked, perhaps told is a better way to say it, to set the table before dinner. My immediate inclination was to resist the order, but I discovered with time that there was a sense of security and order in this task—something that gave me the feeling that I was making an important contribution to the dinner hour.

What I didn't realize at the time was that this "table manner" was one of several that set the stage for good conversation among family members. (How foreign this sounds to a generation that has learned to throw dinner on a TV tray and head for the den.) The dinner hour was a time to exchange information and feelings, a time to converse and listen. In short, it was a time to learn from each other.

As an adult I came to see the importance of what Roland Nelson, at the Center for Creative Leadership in Greensboro, North Carolina, calls "the table manners of leadership." By this he means those small behaviors that facilitate an exchange of information and feelings that leads to learning and better relationships. Stated another way, the table manners of leadership are not used to manipulate people as objects within a bureaucratic hierarchy (Peck, 1993). Rather, they are used to create environments (curricula) where persons can learn from each other in lateral relationships with each other. In the remainder of this section of the chapter, I will discuss the table manners of leadership within school settings that can stimulate learning and better relationships among all within these environments. In the process the leader and others can develop their own curricula.

Entrance and exit rituals are important in any setting. For example, one of the adages in the luxury hotel business is "that if you manage the first and last impressions of a guest properly, then you'll have a happy guest" (Kleinfield, 1989, p. 36). One of the first things hotel workers are told is that eye contact is a necessary behavior for greeting guests when they arrive at the hotel (Kleinfield, 1989). Such contact communicates your willingness to go out of your way to help the person(s) entering the setting, and it says you are risking a certain kind of vulnerability on their behalf.

It has always been amazing to me to watch some leaders use smiles and other nonverbal behaviors to relax persons entering a setting. They also frequently exhibit the ability to establish an affinity connection with so-called small talk.

Leaders who have given attention to entrance rituals know the importance of the physical setting. For example, one school principal inherited a high counter that served as a barrier between guests and the secretary. The counter was removed to facilitate exchange of ideas and feelings. Another principal instructed the secretary and others to always begin conversations with guests by saying "Welcome to *our* school. How may I help you?"

A good energy level on the part of the greeter is important but it is not sufficient in itself. Guests want to know that school leaders have a sense of purpose so that children and adults will be involved in meaningful activity. A clear but concise vision statement communicates this sense of direction: "Everything we do here is aimed at helping children and adults become the best they can be." This general vision statement can be followed by more specific goals for the school.

Principals and others who serve as greeters may profit from knowing the difference between acceptable onstage and backstage behaviors. For example, the person who is counting lunch money would do well to do so in the principal's office rather than in the secretaries' area. This responsibility requires uninterrupted concentration. If the person in charge of counting money considers guests to be an interruption, they will not feel invited into the school. It is good to remind ourselves that some chaos backstage is necessary for an orderly environment onstage (Kleinfield, 1989).

Exit rituals are equally significant. For example, the principal and other adult educators who walk parents and other guests to the door have the opportunity to prolong their conversation and demonstrate their care for the guests. It is an opportunity to summarize what has happened during the visit, thank guests for their interest in the children and the school, and invite them back for another visit.

Exit rituals have demonstrated repeatedly that "there is no more loyal guest than one who has a problem that gets fixed" (Kleinfield, 1989, p. 32). Luxury hotel surveys have also revealed time and again "that guests very much like being called by name" (Kleinfield, 1989, p. 35).

Listening is probably the most powerful civility available to the creative curriculum leader. It is flattering to the speaker and it demonstrates that you aren't self-centered, but instead are eager to learn more about the person speaking. By focusing on the speaker you will also lessen your anxiety (Linver, 1978). By actively listening you will communicate that you understand where the speaker is coming from, and care enough about that person to step into his or her shoes (Linver, 1978). Make no mistake about it, listening is hard work—what M. Scott Peck has called a manifestation of love (Peck, 1978). It relies on the discipline of bracketing, "the temporary giving up or setting aside of one's own prejudices, frames of reference and desires" (Peck, 1978, p. 128). The true listener temporarily communicates total acceptance of the speaker, the result being that the person speaking will feel less threatened and will make himself or herself more vulnerable by telling you more (Peck, 1978).

It is clear from our discussion of the table manners of leadership that the effective leader primarily sees self as learner. The curiosity the effective leader has about other persons, self, and organizational settings will be a driving force in his or her own curriculum development. Growth and learning will oftentimes be their own reward—benefits that far outweigh money and possessions.

Speaking is another critical communicative skill that may be important in learning more about yourself and others. How significant is this skill in comparison to writing? Sandy Linver (1978), author of the best-selling book, *Speakeasy*, answers this question: "The way we interact with other people—both personally and professionally, has very little to do with the written word. It is almost totally based on speaking" (p. 18).

There is no one right speaking style. Rather, a speaker's credibility depends on authenticity or genuineness. It therefore makes sense that the starting place for good speaking is to know what kind of person you basically are.

Please take a moment to complete the following self-inventory. It will give you a start in assessing your comfort and proficiency as a speaker.

How Good (and Comfortable) Are You as a Public Speaker?

Please assess your comfort and proficiency on the following items, from 1 (low) to 5 (high):

	Comfort	Proficiency
1. Speaking one-to-one.		
2. Listening one-to-one.		
3. Answering questions one-to-one.		
4. Speaking to a small group.		
5. Listening (as the speaker/leader) to verbal and nonverbal language of the group.		
6. Answering questions after speaking to a small group.		
7. Speaking to a large group.		
8. Listening (as the speaker/leader) to verbal and nonverbal language in a large group.		
9. Answering questions after speaking to a large group.		
10. Telephone interviews.		
11. Television interviews.		
12. Radio interviews.		
13. Newspaper reporter interviews.		

Are you more comfortable relating to people in formal or informal situations? If your style is more formal, use a podium and stick rather closely to your detailed notes or written speech. If your style is more informal, push the lectern aside and move into the audience as if you were having a conversation. Once again, draw on your "honesty and courage to be authentic with your audience and project to them who you really are" (Linver, 1978, p. 59). One of the best examples of authentic responses was reported in *Time* magazine on January 4, 1993 (p. 55). Television brought the devastation of the Los Angeles riots into every living room, and an unsophisticated man nervously stepped before the camera and said, "Can we all get along?" It was the TV moment of the year.

Regardless of your style, the secret is to focus on the audience, rather than yourself, and share your warmth with them. One good way to focus on the audience is to think about how curious you are to learn more about them and their reaction to your ideas. You will discover that "it's this desire for contact, to make something happen, that gives a speaker energy" (Linver, 1978, p. 41). One way to share your warmth is to share your sense of humor. This has the effect of relaxing the audience, whether it is one person or 100.

My father attended an college alumni meeting in Bradenton, Florida, hundreds of miles away from his alma mater, Albion College, in Michigan. The speaker was the president of the college. My father called me after the speech and raved about the president. "Why did you like him so much?" I asked. Dad responded, "He talked to each of us before the speech about our personal interests in the college and he cared about what we had to say." In short, the president set the stage for his own success before he even spoke a word in the more formal setting. In the process, the president relaxed himself before the speech.

The physical setting in which you speak sets the stage for your speaking. In both formal and informal settings, it can be useful to have a mental checklist. For example, remove distractions, such as a gurgling coffeepot; have chairs and/or tables arranged the way you want them; assess acoustics and check equipment; and have a résumé for the person who is introducing you. Your preparation for the situation sends the message "I care enough about you, the audience, to have done my homework." And good preparation also gives you, the speaker, a sense of security.

You will naturally be nervous to some extent before speaking in many situations. Treat this nervousness as a good thing, for it means that you care enough about the audience and yourself to get psyched up for the occasion. Self-talk can be helpful as you prepare: "Good going. I have an edge on and I know that this is necessary in order to do a good job." It is especially helpful to realize that the audience wants you to succeed and is therefore with you from the start.

As related throughout this book, the audience wants to know what your personal curriculum is and how you have developed it. They want to know where you have been, where you are, and where you want to go in the future. In short, for the audience, *you are the curriculum*. There will obviously be areas of mutual concern if not common experiences. In speaking to this mutuality you will establish an affinity connection.

One of the advantages speaking has over writing is that you get immediate reaction to your ideas. Since 65% of communication is nonverbal body language, you will be able to read your audience and know how your ideas are being received. As you share your warmth with them, they will share their warmth with you.

Because more and more educators are expected to go on television, we have prepared a list of guidelines for this challenge:

1. Talk to the reporter, not the camera or microphone. (Look the reporter straight in the eye.)
2. Stand or sit erectly. Don't stoop or bend over.
3. If you say "No comment," add that you will get back to the reporter by such and such a time.
4. Know who you're dealing with and develop rapport with the reporter when possible.
5. Remember that the good photographer (camera person) doesn't always have the camera to his or her eye. The camera can be rolling from any position, even if it is under his or her arm.
6. Be politely on your guard all of the time.
7. Take advantage of nonconfrontational "good news" programs.
8. The bottom line is to meet reporters head-on and be honest. The camera doesn't lie. It will see the eyes.
9. Be cool and confident. It disarms reporters.
10. Remember that there is a high degree of sensitivity about minorities and women at this time in the history of our nation.
11. A smile is the most disarming thing in the world. Bring to the camera the real person inside you.
12. Be prepared. If you don't know, say "I don't know."

13. There is no such thing as "off-the-record." Beware of the reporter who says, "This is off-the-record."
14. You can ask to talk to the reporter about something before you go on camera. If the reporter won't allow you to do this, don't talk.
15. It is a good idea to suggest a place for the interview. Get an appropriate visual backdrop.
16. Watch hazards around you. Don't swivel in a chair. Don't fidget. Calm down, even if it means that you grab a desk in front of you or behind you.
17. Take your time.
18. Ask to reshoot if you are extremely dissatisfied with the interview.
19. Limit the number of remarks and focus on two or three major points.
20. Ask the reporter who he or she has not only talked to already, but also will talk to before this story is over.
21. You can occasionally stop a reporter dead in his or her tracks by saying, "I have no earthly idea what you're talking about."
22. The school or central office is private property. Be aware, however, that television cameras can "shoot" onto your property from a nearby site without your permission.

Familiarity with television interviews will be enhanced as you have more and more experiences with reporters. How does one get better and better at this? Practice . . . practice . . . practice. "Winston Churchill was asked what he did in his spare time. He responded, 'I rehearse my extemporaneous speeches' " (Adams, 1983, p. 229).

Writing affords you another vehicle for communicating with parents and others interested in schools. Time and time again, parents share with others memos from the principal's office that have serious spelling and grammatical errors. Teachers' comments on student papers also sometimes have such errors. Parents ask, "How can they teach good writing when they don't know what good writing is?"

Correct spelling and grammar are important table manners of leadership. Because we all make spelling and grammatical errors, the secret is to have a proficient copy editor who will proofread our memos and the like. It takes extra effort and time to use a proofreader, but many an embarrassing moment can be avoided with such effort.

An important question to ask in sending a letter or memorandum is, "What is my purpose in doing this?" This purpose should be clearly stated, with concrete next steps spelled out concisely and precisely, so that the parents or other adults know what they are expected to do in response to your communication. In the event that you want to be sure of a response or expedite such a response from an individual, include a stamped, self-addressed envelope.

Finally, always send clean copy. Poorly typed communications and badly photocopied materials send the message that you are sloppy and unprofessional.

Miscellaneous table manners of creative curriculum leadership are as follows:

1. When leaving a message on a telephone answering machine, state your name, telephone number, nature of the business, and the best time to return the call. *State this information slowly.* Remember, the person listening to your request is writing the information down.

2. Before meeting with other persons or having important phone conversations, prepare for the content of the conversation, even if this means writing notes from which you speak.

3. Always give your full name when making a phone call. Many people begin speaking and the other party has no idea who it is.

4. There are two major ways to assure you that you can do something with the support of your "bureaucratic superiors": (a) remove irritants; and (b) be willing to share the credit if efforts are successful, and share the blame if they are not.

5. When substantive agreements are arrived at over the telephone, follow up with a memorandum of understanding, concluding with, "Unless I hear from you otherwise, I'll assume this is correct."

6. Log important contacts with other parties.

We would do well to remind ourselves that all forms of communication are promissory activity (Goffman, 1959, pp. 2-3). We promise that we will act out what we have said we will do. We will, as they say these days, "walk the talk." In more sophisticated academic terms, we will involve ourselves in praxis: reflective action.

Conclusion

The details of creative curriculum leadership, such as the table manners of leadership, are a necessary but insufficient part of the leader's civility. When such details are part of the leader's total character we gauge the effectiveness of the whole person. It has been argued in this book that highly effective leaders view others as precious human beings, whose talents can be identified and used in the creation of settings and organizations. This does not mean that leaders and others always agree. It does mean that they relate to each other with honesty, integrity, and authenticity.

Case 13: Some Upper-Middle-Class Parents Fight to Keep Tracking

After reviewing relevant research and consulting within the field, the new superintendent of schools worked with her staff to design a plan to move the schools away from their system of tracking students. Opposition to this plan began to surface when the school board held hearings on the subject. This opposition was primarily located in the upper-middle class neighborhoods in general, and the country club area in particular. The bottom line for these parents is that they want their children to be in classes with "the nice people"—that is, people like themselves. And, they see their children as having special advantages for entrance into college and the like if tracking is retained.

You have been appointed to a committee of K-12 educators in your system whose members serve to advise the superintendent on this matter. What will your advice be? Please choose the best of the following alternatives:

1. Advise the superintendent to hold firm and implement her plan to move the schools away from the system of tracking students.
2. Advise the superintendent to withdraw the plan for moving the schools away from the system of tracking students.
3. Stay out of the battle. Say and do nothing.

Case 13: Rationales for
the Alternative Responses

1. Tracking is antidemocratic: The rich get richer and the poor get poorer. Those who support tracking want a special advantage for their children. The superintendent is correct in her review of relevant research, for such research doesn't support tracking. In fact more students learn more from classes in which tracking doesn't take place.

2. Ability grouping keeps the gifted students from being cheated by accommodating individual differences and scholastic aptitude. Ability grouping is especially important in English, mathematics, science, and languages. Urge the superintendent of schools to withdraw her proposal to eliminate tracking. Support the upper-middle-class parents who lead the opposition to the superintendent. Since these parents have more experience in using the sources of power known as expertise, charisma, and succorance, they can have greater influence on those with positional authority—namely, the school board. And, these parents have mastered the use of "the table manners of leadership" (civilities) and can use these table manners to get what they want. The difficulties with this response are several: Research doesn't support the continuation of tracking; access to higher level classes is limited for persons from lower socioeconomic classes; and the favored have a feeling of entitlement. Therefore, consider other responses to find a better alternative.

3. To not get involved does conserve your resources. You will also not get hurt if the battle heats up. However, you abdicate your professional responsibilities by not taking a stand. Seek a better response.

Case 14: You Are Asked to Assess
a "Star Teacher" on Your Team

You are new to the school and are asked to join a team of teachers. On your team there is a veteran teacher who is treated as a "star teacher" by the principal and many of the teachers in the school. You notice that the teacher's "stardom" is the result of several factors: The teacher sings in the church choir of a leading church in the city and is a leader in that church; the teacher volunteers for many committees in the school system and serves as the central office's demonstration teacher for workshops; the teacher dresses very well; and the teacher has excellent public relations skills with parents and others in the community.

However, you also notice that the teacher almost never teaches. That is, the teacher writes assignments on the board that keep the students busy, but rarely teaches the subject matter content and does not grade the students' work in completing the assignments. The "star teacher" does not record grades in the grade book, but instead gives the students nothing lower than a C, even though many of the students do not know the material and should receive low or failing marks. Parents do not complain since their children get good grades.

The "star teacher" recently won the school system's Teacher of the Year award, which consisted of a certificate, press coverage, and $5,000. Last year she was a finalist for the Language Arts Teacher of the Year award, although language arts was taught only three times during the year—the days the teacher was observed by the central office language arts consultant.

The "star teacher" is presently up for the Social Studies Teacher of the Year award. The only time social studies was taught during the first 6 months of the school year was the day the principal did the formal evaluation of the teacher. On that day, the teacher reached into the cupboard and distributed Native American costumes that the children used to act out a role-playing exercise.

The social studies consultant from central office asks you to come to the central office to give testimony that will be useful in assessing the "star" teacher's performance.

What will your response be? Please choose from the following alternatives:

1. Simply say to the consultant that you don't have enough information to respond.
2. Assess the "star teacher" by only applauding her polite behaviors and public relations skills—in other words what most people consider civilities.
3. Give an honest evaluation of the "star teacher," including all of the backstage behaviors you have observed.

Case 14: Rationales for the Alternative Responses

1. It is true that you won't help or hurt the "star teacher," but you won't have assumed professional responsibility in the process. You will conserve your resources of time and energy by not getting involved, but the price is too high. Consider other responses.

2. By focusing on her polite behaviors and public relations skills, you will be telling part of the story and will not hurt the teacher's chances for another award. After all, she is only hurting herself in doing what she does. There have been no checks in place, including those the principal could have put there, in the past. This teacher's civilities are making the whole school look better because of her many awards. The appearance of being a winner is more important in our society than being a winner and the "star teacher" is simply reinforcing this norm. The difficulty with this response is that it perpetuates superficiality and incompetence. Consider other responses.

3. An honest assessment may well cause you some difficulties and pain if word of your evaluation reaches other teachers, including the "star teacher." That is, you may be operating at Level 4 or Level 5 on the Commitment Scale/Hierarchy, whereas responses 1 and 2 would keep you at Level 6. (It doesn't make any difference, as past experience indicates. My choice, therefore, is between Tweedledee and Tweedledum.) The payoffs for you in giving an honest assessment are many: (a) You will have the self-esteem that comes with being genuine and doing the right thing, the highest hallmark of civility; (b) you will know that you have been a professional who was willing to censure a colleague, if necessary; and (c) the "star teacher" will not get an award that would further perpetuate her "fraud." This is the best response.

Case 15: You Sense a Need for
Faculty and Students to Learn the
"Table Manners of Leadership"

You are a veteran teacher with a high level of credibility among colleagues. You are on the principal's advisory council and the lead teacher on your teaching team. For some time now you have been concerned about the lack of "table manners of leadership" on the part of some teachers on your staff. For example, they don't listen well to colleagues or support their efforts, but rather simply talk about their own accomplishments. And a few literally don't have table manners during the lunch hour in the cafeteria.

The problem is compounded by the fact that these same teachers aren't setting the example for many of the children in the school. And yet, you feel that children have to learn the "table manners of leadership" if they are to have the chance to succeed in any occupation in life.

What will you do about this matter? Please choose the best of the following alternatives:

1. Go directly to those teachers who have problems in this area of human behavior and, using all of your public relations skills, make your case for improving their "table manners of leadership."
2. Talk to the principal about your concerns and see where you go from there.
3. Go directly to the principal's advisory council and make your concerns known.
4. Put the matter aside and concentrate on other matters as this issue is too sensitive to proceed.

Case 15: Rationales for
the Alternative Responses

1. This response has all of the virtues of any direct action. You will make your views known to the people who have the problem. The difficulty with this approach is that, naturally, those with the problem will probably resent your judgment and resist your efforts to change their behavior. Consider other alternatives.

2. The principal is the formally designated head of the school and as such would probably want to be involved at the front end of any efforts to deal with this issue. Also, the principal is in a position to make things happen without your communicating a "holier than thou" attitude. In all likelihood, the principal will involve the advisory council, and you will play a key role in setting up workshops or the like to deal with this matter. For example, the whole faculty may be invited to hear a flight attendant speak about "the table manners of leadership" taught by airlines. An indirect approach, in this case, has more virtues than drawbacks. This is probably the best response.

3. This is a matter of consequence that will ultimately need to be handled by teachers in the school. It is professional courtesy to involve other teachers at the beginning of this process. There are two major difficulties with this response: (a) The principal will not be involved, thus keeping you from using his or her positional authority at the onset; and (b) colleagues may well feel you are self-righteous or "holier than thou," in which case your credibility will be eroded. Consider other responses.

4. Not stating your views on an issue so important to you is a Lose/Win strategy that could well lead to other problems. Specifically, you may release your anger at those with few "table manners of leadership" in a way that will be detrimental to them and you. Consider better responses.

Case 16: Principal Hears New
Superintendent's Views on Dress

You are having lunch with the new superintendent before the school year begins. The superintendent says, "You can't convince me that people don't sense whether or not you're professional from the minute they see how you're dressed. Good ol' boy principals usually wear short-sleeved shirts, rather than suits or sharp sport coats, and they often wear outdated ties and plaid blazers." Now that you know your new superintendent's views on these matters, how will you act as principal with regard to them? Choose from the following alternative responses or add a better response of your own.

1. A principal's competence is what counts. Does he or she deliver? Dress is a personal and idiosyncratic matter. Continue to dress as you have and advise fellow principals to do likewise.
2. Make minor adjustments in your dress if they are called for. Advise your colleagues to do likewise.
3. Follow the new superintendent's dress code. Advise your colleagues to do likewise.

Case 16: Rationales for the Alternative Explanations

1. Dress is your own business and has nothing to do with success as a principal. You have demonstrated that you have done the job well and people know that. The products of your work are what's really important. Don't openly confront the superintendent, but go about your business as you always have done.

2. You will be a minor irritant on occasion to the superintendent, but you surely won't get into the trouble that you would get into with the first response. Have clothes that are in style, whenever possible, but dress according to what makes you comfortable as much as you can. Be sure to dress appropriately for big occasions when the superintendent wants to show off the staff to the board and the community. Consider the next alternative.

3. Dressing correctly is a small price to pay for the good results you will achieve. Many people will remember the impression you make with your clothes more than anything else. You are more likely to move up the ladder and be a successful administrator if you follow the superintendent's advice. Dress is symbolic, a kind of emotional shorthand, and as such it becomes an important matter to superintendents as they relate to principals. Superintendents want the organization and themselves to look good and appear to be winners.

Case 17: Superintendent Informed of Racist and Sexist Humor Used by a Principal

A teacher informs you that her principal tells racist, sexist, and "dirty" jokes to teachers of both sexes, in a variety of settings. You have personally observed the principal telling "dirty" jokes and have also had confirmation of the teacher's charges from others in the central office. What will you do? Choose from these alternative responses or add a better response of your own.

1. Confront the principal and tell him that racist and sexist humor can get him fired, and you want no more of it on his part. Overlook the "dirty" jokes. Talk to him about these jokes only if you hear another complaint from a person of the opposite sex.

2. Overlook the matter and just go about your business as superintendent of schools.

3. Confront the principal and tell him that racist and sexist humor as well as "dirty" jokes are inappropriate and will hurt his professional image as well as the image of the school and school system. Follow up with a memorandum that makes your position a matter of public record in the event that you are ever confronted about the matter.

4. Have your assistant superintendent, who works directly with principals, deal with this matter. Be sure you are informed as to how the matter is handled. In this way you won't experience the downside of being directly involved. That is, the assistant superintendent will be held accountable for the situation.

Case 17: Rationales for the Alternative Responses

1. You are wise to confront the principal so that he gets straight signals on the matter of racist and sexist humor. It can get both of you in trouble and therefore must be addressed immediately. So-called dirty jokes are an affinity connection or kind of male bonding mechanism. Just be sure that the principal understands that such jokes are not to be told in front of women. Please choose again.

2. People are always complaining about something, and these days they are supersensitive about matters like these. After all, school board members sometimes tell off-color jokes as a way to bond and relax. Please choose again.

3. This is probably the best response. People are naturally more sensitive to issues of racism and sexism, and the courts reflect this sensitivity. All educators must understand that inappropriate humor

is simply that. Remember, you are the model for all educators in the system.

4. Delegation of responsibility is the hallmark of an effective superintendent. You shouldn't have to take the heat on all matters, and this matter serves as a case in point. The difficulty is that delegation in this case is in effect a missed opportunity for you to let all principals know your stand on this important matter. This is why the previous response is probably better.

APPENDIX A

A Personal Change and Conservation Inventory

_____ (My Name)

What are the three things about *my leadership* that I highly value and want to conserve?

1. _____

2. _____

3. _____

What are the three things about *my leadership* that I want to change—challenges?

1. _____

2. _____

3. _____

APPENDIX B

An Organizational Change and Conservation Inventory

_____ (Name of Your Organization)

What are three things about *your organization* that you highly value and want to conserve?

1. _____

2. _____

3. _____

What are three things about *your organization* that you want to change?

1. _____

2. _____

3. _____

APPENDIX C

Traits of Outstanding Leaders

After experiencing a situation in which I felt a leader was "brilliant," students were asked to tell a story about an experience they had when an administrator/leader was "brilliant" or "superior." We then listed the qualities of the leader at that time. Please use the following as a checklist to characterize a leader who was "brilliant" or "superior" in a situation you've experienced:

___ 1. Used applied intelligence (high-level common sense).

___ 2. Was authoritative (had a sense of presence).

___ 3. Did his/her homework (facts + frameworks/context).

___ 4. An expert planner—left situation with concrete next steps in mind.

___ 5. Sense of purpose (vision) stated clearly and referred to when appropriate. Clearly committed.

___ 6. Listened well and spoke to persons at their level.

___ 7. Fair.

___ 8. Authentic or genuine (not phony).

___ 9. Compassionate (not patronizing) and sensitive.

___ 10. Not mean-spirited. Has a sense of humor.

___ 11. Willing to take risks (make self vulnerable).

___ 12. Trusts (able to "bracket" self and look at situation as if objective).

___ 13. Good of organization a primary consideration.

___ 14. Able to build partnerships.

Sources of Power Available to the Creative Curriculum Leader

positional authority

expertise

charisma

succorance

Effective Communication

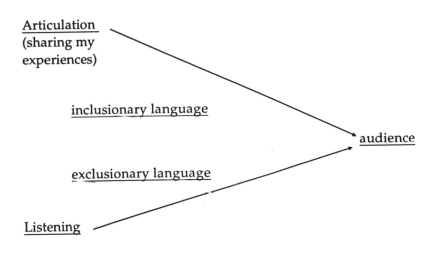

Articulation
(sharing my
experiences)

inclusionary language

audience

exclusionary language

Listening

selective

true (total attention—role of "bracketing")

References

Adams, J. G. (1983). *Without precedent*. New York: Horton.

Attinger, J. (1992, March 9). Steinem: Tying politics to the personal. *Time*, p. 55.

Austin, G. (1993). Conversation with the author.

Austin, G., & Brubaker, D. (1988). Making the right calls. *Piedmont Airlines, 15*, pp. 103-105.

Bly, R. (1990). *Iron John*. Reading, MA: Addison-Wesley.

Bogdan, R. L., & Biklen, S. (1982). *Qualitative research for education*. Boston: Allyn & Bacon.

Bogen, J. (1979). Some educational aspects of hemispheric specialization. *Dromenon, 1*, 16-21.

Brubaker, D. (1967). *Alternative directions for the social studies*. Scranton, PA: International Textbook Co.

Brubaker, D. (1979). *Who's teaching—Who's learning?* Santa Monica, CA: Goodyear.

Brubaker, D. (1982). *Curriculum planning: The dynamics of theory and practice*. Glenview, IL: Scott, Foresman.

Brubaker, D. (1986, August 3). There's no substitute for wanting to be there. *Greensboro News & Record*, p. E3.

Brubaker, D. (1988, October 8). Leadership: Antidote to boredom, cynicism. *The Salisbury Post*, p. 8.

Brubaker, D. (1989). A curriculum leader's search for meaning. *Journal of Instruction Psychology, 16*, 107-111.

Brubaker, D. (1992). The underpinnings of creative leadership. *National Forum of Educational Administration and Supervision Journal*, 9, 4-11.

Brubaker, D., & Kinard, L. (1988, July 10). Let the "fire" inside express itself. *Greensboro News & Record*, p. E3.

Brubaker, D., & Nelson, R. (1974). *Creative survival in educational bureaucracies*. Berkeley, CA: McCutchan.

Brubaker, D., & Simon, L. (1993). *Teacher as decision maker*. Newbury Park, CA: Corwin Press.

Buber, M. (1970). *I and thou*. New York: Scribner.

Buckley, W. (1976). *Airborne*. Boston: Little, Brown.

Buckley, W. (1982). *Atlantic high*. Boston: Little, Brown.

Callahan, S. (1986). *Adrift*. New York: Ballantine.

Combs, A., Avila, D., & Purkey, W. (1971). *Helping relationships*. Boston: Allyn & Bacon.

Covey, S. (1989). *The 7 habits of highly effective people*. New York: Simon & Schuster.

Deford, F. (1992, April 20). Arthur Ashe's secret. *Newsweek*, pp. 62-63.

Dreyfuss, R. (1986, March 23). Interview. *Parade Magazine*, pp. 6-7.

DuVall, L. (1989, February 4). Speech to graduate students in Educational Administration, Higher Education and Research, the University of North Carolina at Greensboro.

Eisner, E. W. (1988). The primacy of experience and the politics of method. *Educational Researcher*, 17, 15-20.

Emerson, R. W. (1903). *Essays on history, nature, addresses and lectures*. Boston: Beacon.

Fox, M. (1983). *Original blessing*. Sante Fe, NM: Bear.

Gerth, H., & Mills, C. W. (1946). *From Max Weber: Essays in sociology*. New York: Oxford.

Gibran, K. (1923). *The prophet*. New York: Knopf.

Goffman, E. (1959). *The presentation of self in everyday life*. New York: Doubleday Anchor.

Greene, M. (1975). Curriculum and consciousness. In W. Piner (Ed.), *Curriculum theorizing: The reconceptualists* (pp. 299-317). Berkeley, CA: McCutchan.

Habermas, J. (1971). *Knowledge and human interests*. Boston: Beacon.

Hedrick, D. (1993, June 29). The interview. Unpublished paper. Greensboro: The University of North Carolina at Greensboro.

Hutschnecker, A. (1974). *The drive for power.* New York: Evans.

Jackson, P. (1986). *The practice of teaching.* New York: Teachers College Press.

James, W. (1979). *The will to believe.* Cambridge, MA: Harvard University Press. (Original work published 1897)

Kleinfield, S. (1989). *The hotel.* New York: Simon & Schuster.

Lightfoot, S. (1983). *The good high school.* New York: Basic Books.

Linver, S. (1978). *Speakeasy.* New York: Summit.

Macdonald, J. B. (1977, December). Interview conducted by Ruth Fairfield at the University of North Carolina at Greensboro.

Macdonald, J. B. (1980). Curriculum theory as intentional activity. *Humanistic Education Project Paper No. 20* (pp. 1-6). Greensboro: University of North Carolina at Greensboro.

May, R. (1972). *Power and innocence.* New York: Norton.

May, R. (1975). *The courage to be.* New York: Bantam.

McCall, M., Lombardo, M., & Morrison, A. (1988). *The lessons of experience.* Lexington, MA: Lexington Books.

Peck, M. S. (1978). *The road less traveled.* New York: Simon & Schuster.

Peck, M. S. (1993). *A world waiting to be born: Civility rediscovered.* New York: Bantam.

Pinar, W. (1975). The analysis of educational experience. In W. Pinar (Ed.), *Curriculum theorizing: The reconceptualists* (pp. 384-395). Berkeley, CA: McCutchan.

Sarason, S. (1971). *The culture of the school and the problem of change.* Boston: Allyn & Bacon.

Sarason, S. (1972). *The creation of settings and the future societies.* San Francisco: Jossey-Bass.

Sarason, S. (1993a). *The case for change.* San Francisco: Jossey-Bass.

Sarason, S. (1993b). *Letters to a serious education president.* Newbury Park, CA: Corwin Press.

Schein, E. (1985). *Organizational culture and leadership.* San Francisco: Jossey-Bass.

Shcharansky, A. (1986, February 24). Visit with a survivor. *Time,* p. 38.

Smith, H. (1988). *The power game.* New York: Random House.

Steinbeck, J. (1952). *East of Eden.* New York: Penguin.

Steinem, G. (1992). *Revolution from within: A book of self-esteem.* Boston: Little, Brown.

Tillich, P. (1952). *The courage to be.* New Haven: Yale University Press.

Toffler, A. (1980). The third wave. New York: Bantam.

Tyler, R. (1949). *Basic principles of curriculum and instruction.* Chicago: The University of Chicago Press.

Welsh, P. (1987). *Tales out of school.* New York: Penguin.

Yinger, R. (1978). A study of teacher planning: Description and preactive decision making. *Research Series, 18* (The Institute for Research on Teaching at Michigan State University), 4, 8.

Author Index

Subject Index

DATE DUE

FEB 28 '98		
APR 0 3 2000		
7-30-01		
OCT 2 4 2001		
AP 10 '02		
1/02/03		
11/12/10		
GAYLORD		PRINTED IN U.S.A